'This book must have been a labour of love – a comprehensive view of grants fundraising based on solid research a[…] successful trust fundraiser. It's all here: the h[…] life examples. If you need a friendly guide to […] book for you.'
Alex Blake, Director, KEDA Consulting

'*Grants Fundraising* is a treasure trove of fur[…] approachable and engaging style. It is essential for anyone who is looking to establish a modern and profitable grants fundraising programme.

Neela Jane shows how grants fundraising has changed over the years, with relationships now centre stage. She debunks the myths of this much misunderstood discipline and shares case studies – addressing both success and failure – which provide a fascinating insight into real-world fundraising. The generosity of Neela Jane and her contributors will help others looking to follow them on the path to success.'
Caroline Danks, LarkOwl

'This guide captures the essence of successful grants fundraising and is so well written the practical and well-informed advice jumps off the page. I also love the thoughtful analogies, examples and case studies that add depth to the information. If fundraisers follow Neela Jane's wise suggestions, they will succeed.'
Amanda Delew, Director, Solid Management and Consultancy Services

'Great content, amazing tips, fabulous insights... What a wonderful read! This book will certainly be an asset to anyone looking to secure grants funding and increase income for their organisation. In an increasingly competitive world of seeking support from grant-making trusts and foundations, fundraisers need to hone their skills and knowledge – this book will help you to do this.'
Gill Jolly, Director, Achieve Consultants Ltd

'This is a fantastic how-to guide on fundraising from foundations and other funders, taking the reader step-by-step through a thorough process that will maximise your chances of successful grant fundraising. Neela Jane clearly knows her stuff and has tons of practical suggestions for developing those all-important relationships with your current and potential funders.'
Carol Mack, Chief Executive, Association of Charitable Foundations

'A great guide to fundraising from grant-makers. Engaging and practical, this book provides a brilliant grounding in the art of relationship-based fundraising. A highly recommended read for any trust fundraiser!'
Geraldine Payne,

'Neela Jane provides a complete 360-degree view of grants fundraising. With fresh and welcome perspectives on what grant-makers as well as grant-seekers want, the author calls out complaints that success is more about luck than judgement or that any efforts are dogged by power imbalances.

The book abounds with useful guidance and tools, including templates for the planning process, links to further resources and, crucially, advice on key issues such as data protection compliance. I strongly recommend it to all fundraisers aiming at a strong and more sustainable fundraising base for their organisation.'
Cathy Pharoah, Visiting Professor of Charity Funding, Bayes Business School, City, University of London

'This gem of a book is a must-have for grant-seekers of all levels of expertise. Covering the basics for those new to the world of grants fundraising, it also contains a whole host of tips and advice for even the most experienced fundraisers.'
Natalie Prosser, Grove Cottage (Bishop's Stortford Mencap)

'Neela Jane's book outlines all the necessary steps to conceive, plan and execute a successful grants fundraising programme. Clear and pragmatic principles are backed up by case studies and examples, putting the theory into real-life context. This is an essential read for those relatively new to building relationships with trusts and foundations and those that manage grants fundraising in their organisation. It is also useful to trustees, so they might better grasp the conditions under which fundraisers operate.'
Stuart Sherriff, CEO, Gryphon Research Ltd

'Full of practical tips and colourful examples, this guide draws on the experience of many successful fundraisers alongside with Neela Jane's own expertise. It is as helpful a reminder on best practice for a seasoned fundraiser as it is a step-by-step manual for someone setting out to raise money from grants for the first time.'
Beth Upton, CEO, Money Tree Fundraising

'I loved this book! Neela Jane has written a practical guide full of helpful tips, tools and examples to help you build relationships with trusts and foundations and to succeed in the complex world of fundraising. Whether you're just starting out or you've got some fundraising experience and want to keep improving, this book is full of ideas that will help.'
Rob Woods, Author and Fundraising Trainer

The Fundraising Series

Grants Fundraising

Neela Jane Stansfield

dsc
directory of social change

In association with:
University of Kent | Centre for Philanthropy
Chartered Institute of Fundraising

Published by the Directory of Social Change (Registered Charity no. 800517 in England and Wales)

Office: Suite 103, 1 Old Hall Street, Liverpool L3 9HG

Tel: 020 4526 5995

Visit www.dsc.org.uk to find out more about our books, subscription funding website and training events. You can also sign up for e-newsletters so that you're always the first to hear about what's new.

The publisher welcomes suggestions and comments that will help to inform and improve future versions of this and all of our titles. Please give us your feedback by emailing publications@dsc.org.uk.

Print and digital editions first published 2022

ISBN 978 1 78482 064 0 (print edition)
ISBN 978 1 78482 065 7 (digital edition)

British Library Cataloguing in Publication Data
A catalogue record for this book is available from the British Library

Cover and text design by Kate Griffith
Typeset by Marlinzo Services, Frome
Printed and bound in Great Britain by CPI Group, Croydon

To my Dad, who has spent his life making the world a better place and encouraging us to try to do the same.

And to Chris, who makes it better just by being in it.

Contents

About the Fundraising Series

For hundreds, if not thousands, of years generous people have given of their resources to improve the lives of others. Underpinning that benevolence are the people who ask for support on behalf of causes and for those in need – the fundraisers. As a group, they are often little known and little celebrated, but they are a driving force in enabling others to express their philanthropy and experience the joy of giving.

Over the last century or so, fundraisers' work has become more and more professionalised. The role of the fundraiser is achieving professional recognition through the establishment of the Chartered Institute of Fundraising (CIoF), the development of fundraising education and a growing interest in codifying professional ethics. Rightly, fundraisers are increasingly acknowledged as having a particular set of skills, and their knowledge base is growing in size and scope.

This series aims to help fundraisers build their skills and grow professionally. Each volume addresses a key part in the spectrum of fundraising techniques. As fundraising evolves and develops, new titles in the series are added and old ones revised. Each title explores a particular fundraising activity: looks at the current best practice; helps establish future strategy; and, where relevant, considers the historical, ethical and theoretical context for that activity. The series offers something for anyone who is aspiring to be a professional fundraiser, whatever the size or type of their organisation or the stage of their career.

The Centre for Philanthropy at the University of Kent is proud to partner with the Directory of Social Change and CIoF in the development of the series, as part of our shared mission to open up insights from the academic world to practising fundraisers. We'd also like to pay tribute to fundraising academic Adrian Sargeant for his early championing and stewardship of the series.

This series wouldn't be possible without the hard work of many people from authors to contributors to the publishing team who shape the text; we thank everyone who has contributed to its development.

Dr Claire Routley
Dr Beth Breeze
Centre for Philanthropy
University of Kent

About the Directory of Social Change

At the Directory of Social Change (DSC), we believe that the world is made better by people coming together to serve their communities and each other. For us, an independent voluntary sector is at the heart of that social change and we exist to support charities, voluntary organisations and community groups in the work they do. Our role is to:

- **provide practical information** on a range of topics from fundraising to project management in both our printed publications and our e-books;
- **offer training** through public courses, events and in-house services;
- **research funders** and maintain a subscription database, *Funds Online*, with details on funding from grant-making charities, companies and government sources;
- **offer bespoke research** to voluntary sector organisations in order to evaluate projects, identify new opportunities and help make sense of existing data;
- **stimulate debate and campaign** on key issues that affect the voluntary sector, particularly to champion the concerns of smaller charities.

We are a registered charity ourselves but we self-fund most of our work. We charge for services, but cross-subsidise those which charities particularly need and cannot easily afford.

Visit our website **www.dsc.org.uk** to see how we can help you to help others and have a look at **www.fundsonline.org.uk** to see how DSC could improve your fundraising. Alternatively, call our friendly team at **020 4526 5995** to chat about your needs or drop us a line at **cs@dsc.org.uk**.

About the author

Neela Jane Stansfield is a major gifts fundraising specialist, with over 15 years' experience working with trusts, foundations and high-net-worth individuals. She is an Associate at Fundraising Training Ltd and has worked across the international development, health and education sectors, including at UNICEF UK, Marie Curie, the Stroke Association and Chatteris Educational Foundation in Hong Kong.

For six years, Neela Jane was Chair of the Trusts and Statutory Special Interest Group at the Chartered Institute of Fundraising (CIoF), leading a membership body of 4,000 grants fundraisers across the UK. She was also a board member and speaker for several years at the CIoF National Convention – the largest fundraising conference in Europe.

She holds a BSc in Psychology from the University of Nottingham and a diploma in fundraising from the CIoF, and has written about trusts and major gifts fundraising for *Third Sector* magazine and *The Guardian*'s Voluntary Sector Network. She has also been a trustee for an international children's charity, Children in Crisis, and is currently a trustee for ATLEU – the Anti-Trafficking and Labour Exploitation Unit, working to provide safety, recovery and redress for victims of trafficking and modern slavery.

Neela Jane lives in Devon with her husband and three little people. In her spare time she loves going for a run (and taking part in the odd charity marathon), playing the piano and hiding in the cupboard eating chocolate biscuits when the kids aren't looking.

Acknowledgements

This book would not have been possible without the input and support of many wonderful people.

Firstly, hugest thanks to John Martin and Gabi Zagnojute at the Directory of Social Change, for their fantastic help throughout and for asking me to write it in the first place! It has been such an enjoyable process working with you both, and with Hazel Bird (copy-editor extraordinaire).

A big thank you to Michael Norton and Mike Eastwood, who kindly lent the ideas from their book *Writing Better Fundraising Applications*, which was initially written thirty years ago. Much of the content of their book remains very relevant today and has been largely built upon within these chapters, particularly those looking at proposal development. I hope this book does justice to your original and brilliant work.

I am also indebted to Bill Bruty, who, as well as kindly writing the foreword, provided a plethora of research material to back up the ideas within these pages. I first met Bill as a graduate participant on his Grant-seeker Programme and more recently have had the pleasure of working alongside him at Fundraising Training Ltd. Just as he did those 15 or so years ago, he continues to inspire and make fundraising a lot of fun. Thank you for being such a support, Bill – you are often called a fundraising guru, and it's my privilege to also call you a great mentor and friend.

Huge thanks to a number of other sector associates, colleagues and friends who have kindly taken the time to read and comment on various chapters, making them all the better: Kerry Rock, Mathew Iredale and Paul Ticher provided invaluable support to the research chapters; Rob Woods kindly lent some fantastic ideas to the stewardship section; and Geraldine Payne, Gill Jolly and Natalie Prosser deserve particular recognition for their role as peer reviewers for the entire script – thank you so much for your input and encouragement.

Thank you also to the fundraisers and grant-makers that contributed commentaries, anecdotes and quotes throughout the book, sharing their invaluable experience for the benefit of other charities: ABF – the Soldiers' Charity, the Association of Charitable Foundations, Barrow Cadbury Trust, Best Beginnings, Cancer Research UK, Changing Faces, Charles Hicks, David Bull CBE, Edith Murphy Foundation, Esmée Fairbairn Foundation, Essex Community Foundation, The RUH Charitable Fund, the Institute for Voluntary Action Research, International Justice Mission UK, Lloyds Bank Foundation, Macmillan Cancer Support, The National Lottery Community Fund, NSPCC, Rachel Hunnybun, the Open

University, Paul Hamlyn Foundation, Sported, St John Ambulance, Sue Ryder, Trust for London and UNICEF UK.

Similarly, thank you to the wonderful grants fundraising community, many of whom kindly submitted their questions and challenges to inform the final chapter of this book; I have tried – and I hope succeeded! – to incorporate the answers to all of them at least somewhere within the book.

Finally, the biggest thank you goes to my husband Chris for his unfailing support and for encouraging me to take on this project even while we relocated across the country, moved house twice and had another baby all within the same year! You are a rockstar.

Foreword

Having been a fundraiser for over 35 years, for causes as varied as human rights in Tanzania and addressing the housing crisis in Manchester, I am passionate about grant-seeking. What other job can involve such fascinating journeys into the lives and motivations of the world's great philanthropists, while developing a thorough knowledge of and passion for the projects you are fundraising for? There are few other ways of fundraising that require such research and understanding of the cause and the donors, which is also rewarded by the relatively large size of the gifts.

Speaking truth to power and stimulating a moral response to a social issue is rewarding enough, but when there is a transfer of wealth that helps to address the problem in question too, the feeling is quite exhilarating – having savoured it once there is no turning back. In this definitive guide, Neela Jane shares her recipe for successful grant-seeking. It is based upon a non-judgemental and sincere understanding of the donors, mastery of the research skills and careful consideration of how you will reach your donors. Most grants are agreed between people where there is mutual understanding and respect, before any written proposal is even developed. After all, grant-seeking is not an accidental game.

Unlike many other guides on this subject, this book places the written proposal in its correct place. As it is the most tangible part of the process, we tend to become fixated on the importance of the proposal being perfect. But the final proposal document is merely the result of so much that has to be done in advance for any application to be read, let alone be successful. This book is bristling with proven techniques to ensure that your application will be eligible, accurate and memorable.

Although having been awarded a grant might feel like your work is done, Neela Jane reminds us that thanking, fulfilling your commitments and looking after donors is an essential phase of the grant-seeking journey.

This book is grounded in a profound belief in the justice inherent in grants fundraising. It should not be about self-effacing supplicants quietly grateful for money arriving from outside their communities. This is about informed partnerships and working together as equals to make our world a better place. We don't have to feel humble or apologetic for being fundraisers in search of a more just world.

Bill Bruty FCIoF
Director, Fundraising Training Ltd

CHAPTER ONE

Grants fundraising in context

Introduction

Fundraising from grant-makers has long been big business for the charity sector, with around £3.5 billion of UK annual voluntary income coming from trusts and foundations alone.[1] That's almost one-sixth of all private giving to charities in the UK every year,[2] making it a major funding source upon which charities often heavily rely. The number of grant-makers around the world grows year on year,[3] which is wonderful news for the future of charities and philanthropy. However, so too grows the number of grant-seekers. As well as traditional charities, other organisations now look for support from the same pots, with private and public sector bodies such as the NHS and a range of social enterprises vying for funds. Grants fundraising is therefore more competitive today than it has ever been and, consequently, perhaps all the more compelling.

Since the 2000s, economic ups and downs have had a huge effect on the sector. Financial recessions, banking crises, Brexit and the global COVID-19 pandemic have all significantly impacted charities from small to large, affecting their viability, their operational capacity and of course their ability to generate income. Both grant-makers and grant-seekers have played important parts in sustaining charities during these times, the former frequently coming to the aid of their grant recipients when required and the latter working to keep the lifeblood of their organisations flowing.

The funder–recipient relationship is therefore a critical one, needing careful attention and management. As we will see throughout this book, successful grants fundraising requires several stages and processes to give your charity the best chance of a long-lasting and mutually beneficial funding partnership. Before we dive into these processes, it is helpful to take a look at the types of grant-maker we are talking about and where this important part of the charity sector has its roots.

Terminology: what's in a name?

The words used in grants fundraising can be as varied, and sometimes as confusing, as the diversity of funding itself. Different organisations may use particular terms or phrases in the way they talk about the money they give or raise (and how they go about giving or raising it), depending on which part of the sector they are in and which part of the world they operate in. For the purposes of this book, we will stick to particular words for simplicity, but it is worth noting the various other terms that are widely used in the sector.

Grant-makers

This book predominantly uses the term 'grant-makers', or 'funders' for a little variety. This is simply because the range of grant-making organisations out there is enormous, and yet the processes explored in the following chapters are relevant to almost all types. Grant-makers, as described here, are organisations that fund charitable activities, whether these are a charity's core running costs, specific projects or direct services to help individuals. Grant-makers therefore include charitable trusts and foundations, institutional funding bodies, statutory funding pots, people who give via family foundations and, increasingly, companies that fund charities through their own corporate foundations. Essentially, grant-making in this context includes any organisation that usually requires a proposal as part of its distribution of charitable grants.

In the UK, grant-makers often use the terms 'charitable trust' and 'charitable foundation' in reference to themselves fairly interchangeably. In practice, 'trust' is a term used more within the UK and 'foundation' tends to be more widely used in the USA and across Europe. Other commonly used names are 'settlement' and 'charity' (for example, The ABC Charitable Settlement or The XYZ Charity), but these are generally synonymous with trusts and foundations and the variation usually stems from the different ways they were originally set up. To further complicate the picture, not all trusts and foundations actually make grants; some use their income to finance their own charitable operations and some do grant-making alongside their own service delivery. Throughout the book, therefore, you will find 'grant-makers' and 'funders' used in reference to those that distribute grants to other charities, and 'grant-seekers' and 'fundraisers' used in reference to those that seek out their support.

Proposals

There are lots of different words for a written fundraising proposition, but for ease we will use the word 'proposal'. The terms 'application', 'appeal' or 'case for support' could just as easily be used (although 'case for support' can also refer to a more generalised document) and indeed are often used quite interchangeably by both funders and fundraisers alike. Some may argue that applications are more formal and detailed documents, and that proposals are a briefer overview of an organisation or project's funding needs. Others might contest that the words are dependent upon the style and geographical location of the funder – that UK grant-makers tend to refer to applications and those in the USA talk more about proposals. Others again may prefer to use different terms altogether, such as 'bid', perhaps to describe a more programmatic style of proposal-writing. Really, it's all much of a muchness and we are all talking about the same thing: the method through which we request financial support from a funding body.

Grants

Attempts to define grants bring up interesting questions. In some contexts the terms 'grant' and 'donation' may seem synonymous, but to grant-makers that is not always the case. Many grant-makers consider a donation to be a charitable gift free of any terms or conditions but deem a grant to have particular requirements attached to it, such as how it may be spent and within what time frame. Grants are often more strategic and may come with reporting requirements, even if they are not restricted to a specific project. Grants are also generally more significant in size and require a level of tracking and management specific to the funder's needs and interests.

If this is all a little befuddling, don't worry. The point really is that organisations (and indeed different departments of different organisations!) use a range of words and phrases to describe the grant-making process. Thankfully, as we will explore, there are commonalities in the ways fundraisers can go about their work.

A brief history of grant-making

With so many different types of funder out there, there is also great variety in the history behind them. Some areas of grant-making have become more prominent over the past few decades, such as giving by corporate foundations as vehicles of corporate social responsibility (CSR). In contrast, other more traditional grant-makers have very long and detailed histories. Certainly in the UK, a great number of charitable trusts and foundations were set up prior to the twentieth century. For example, the database of grant-making organisations held by the Directory of Social Change (DSC) includes over a hundred funders set up prior to the early 1900s.[4] Many of them have established a legacy of enriching the lives of their beneficiaries across several decades and even centuries.

Grant-makers exist to give money away, and are usually set up in a way that enables a very tax-efficient method of philanthropy. In the UK, grant-makers that are registered charities can take advantage of tax relief not just on donations they receive but also on their investment income, as well as on any corporation or inheritance tax.[5] There can also be business rates reliefs if they run their own office, making tax efficiency a key part of the decision to set up as a charitable organisation. Tax exemption and tax avoidance should not be confused, however. Grant-makers have historically been set up primarily as a means of distributing charitable support, often based on a deep-rooted passion for helping others in need, with tax relief a welcome aid to these endeavours.

Case study: the history of the Barrow Cadbury Trust

There are many great examples of grant-makers that have a long and rich history, particularly within their local community, and whose origins continue to play an influential role in their grant-making today. A good example of one of these is the Barrow Cadbury Trust.

Barrow Cadbury was a grandson of John Cadbury, founder of the family-run confectionary company in Birmingham. Barrow was working for the family firm when he met Geraldine Southall at a Quaker Meeting House, and the pair married in 1891.

Following their marriage, Barrow and Geraldine gave generously to a great number of charities, particularly those addressing poverty and social injustice in and around Birmingham, in line with their Quaker beliefs. Geraldine was involved in setting up the second juvenile court in the world in 1905, the provision of which became mandatory in the Children Act of 1908, and in 1910 the couple built the Birmingham Children's Remand Home, the UK's first purpose-built home for children due to be brought before the magistrates. Geraldine personally oversaw the individual case of each child who passed through the premises.

The couple established the Barrow and Geraldine S. Cadbury Trust in 1920. They were inspired by Quaker social advocates among their peers, such as Joseph Rowntree (who established the Joseph Rowntree Charitable Trust), and by other Cadbury family trusts which shared many of the same aims and values. At this time, around the end of the First World War, a sharp rise in taxation had led many philanthropists to transform their charitable giving. For families such as the Cadburys, setting up a trust enabled them to direct their business profits more efficiently to the causes they believed in. Barrow was clear that he did not view this wealth as his own; rather, he deemed that it had been entrusted to him for the benefit of society.

As Barrow increasingly succeeded in his roles at Cadbury Brothers Limited, so further capital was transferred to grow the trust. During the 1920s and 1930s, the trust funded numerous causes, including social welfare, health and the building of several open-air schools. The last of these was inspired by Barrow and Geraldine's own experience when their son, Paul, recovered from tuberculosis after greater exposure to fresh air.

After Geraldine died in 1941, the trust continued to express her and Barrow's beliefs, and the couple's three grown-up children served as trustees. After Barrow's death in 1958, Paul Cadbury took over as chair to shape the trust's activities, alongside his own Paul S. Cadbury Trust. Upon Paul's death in 1984, the two trusts were amalgamated to form the Barrow Cadbury Trust.

Today the trust is based in London with a mixed board of family and non-family trustees and a significant office of staff. The trust is now a social investor as well as a grant-maker and campaigner, remaining true to the original vision and values of Barrow and Geraldine in its approach, which is to tackle the underlying root causes of social problems. Its fascinating history is a great example of that which lies behind many of the key funders of charities today, both large and small.[6]

From the 1950s onwards, the UK saw a dramatic rise in the number of charitable trusts being set up. This was in part due to the work of the Committee of Enquiry into the Law and Practice Relating to Charitable Trusts (known as the Nathan Committee), which in 1952 reported on the need for funders to have a means of knowing about each other in order to better benefit the community.[7] The Charities Act 1960 supported this shift by establishing the Central Register of Charities, held at the Charity Commission in London, which made the existence of these funders and their grant-making activities public.

In 1968, the sound of fundraisers rejoicing could be heard up and down the country as the first edition of *The Directory of Grant Making Trusts* was published by the Charities Aid Foundation, detailing the contact details, interests and financial activities of grant-makers in the UK. In 2001 DSC took over the reins for subsequent editions, which have remained a staple in the arsenal of grant-seekers ever since. While this publication was great news for fundraising charities, it was understandably a little less well received by grant-makers, which now found themselves overwhelmed with funding proposals. While some found this transparency reduced the numbers of misguided requests, others subsequently insisted that their listings include the wording 'the trustees will not consider unsolicited applications' – a well-known phrase commonly used to this day.

By the late 1980s, greater recognition of the importance of funder–grantee relations was emerging, as the sector became progressively professionalised. Grant-makers increasingly hired staff, particularly those with expertise in sociological issues, to inform and direct their giving priorities, and in 1989 the Association of Charitable Foundations (ACF) was founded. ACF is the professional membership body for grant-makers in the UK and provides policy advice, advocacy, research and information as well as a range of conferences and seminars for its 400 members.[8] With the growth of this professionalism and increases in the support available to the sector, the relationship between funders and grantees in the UK has gradually become more akin to that seen in philanthropy across the pond.

Grant-makers in the USA have historically been professional and business-like in their approach. Back in 1956, the Foundation Center was established in New York to collect and communicate information on US philanthropy and to act as the key professional association for grant-makers across the country. In 2019, the Foundation Center merged with Guidestar, one of the world's largest sources of information about non-profit organisations, to create the new organisation Candid. Candid has a huge staff base and a highly influential leadership, with the board made up of many of the top names in US grant-making.

In the USA today, grant-makers give over $80 billion every year to charitable causes.[9] US foundations have a particularly strong root in American philanthropy, aided by the early examples of people such as John D. Rockefeller and Andrew Carnegie, who amassed great fortunes and then gave them away through their own now famous philanthropic foundations. Today the largest foundation in the USA is the Gates Foundation, founded by Bill and Melinda Gates, who made their fortune through the company Microsoft. At the time of writing, the foundation has given away over $50 billion in grants to health and poverty-relieving programmes around the world.[10]

Private foundations in the USA are tax exempt under a section of the country's Internal Revenue Code called 501(c)(3). Unlike in the UK, each year they are required to spend 5% of their capital or endowment fund on charitable purposes, as well as 85% of their net income. There are almost 120,000 registered foundations in the USA.[11] They make up a hugely important part of the American charity sector and fund all kinds of charitable work both domestically and around the world.

The USA remains the world's largest marketplace for foundations,[12] but the past few decades have also seen the emergence of many and significant grant-makers across Africa, Asia (particularly China and India), Europe, Latin America and the Middle East. In Europe, an estimated €60 billion is given annually by around 147,000 foundations, with Germany, Italy, the Netherlands, Spain and Switzerland having particularly affluent philanthropy markets.[13] The European Foundation Centre (EFC) was established in 1989 to provide information, research and data for its membership body of philanthropic organisations in over 30 countries. In 2021, EFC merged with Donors and Foundations Networks in Europe (DAFNE) to form the new organisation Philea – Philanthropy Europe Association. The growing plethora of grant-makers across all continents is funding important charitable work across the globe.

Types of grant-maker

In the UK today there are about 12,500 grant-making trusts and foundations.[14] These range from small, local community trusts to huge players on the global philanthropy platform such as the Wellcome Trust, which alone gives away hundreds of millions every year and is the UK's largest foundation at the time of writing.[15] In fact, almost a third of all grants given in the charity sector are by the top ten largest funders.[16]

In addition to traditional charitable trusts and foundations, the marketplace is becoming ever more complex across the different funder types. Some trusts are actually subsidiaries. These have their own names but are donor-advised funds managed by a charitable organisation (such as the Charities Aid Foundation or UK Community Foundations), which looks after the set-up and administration of the fund on behalf of the funder, instead of a separate entity being registered with the charity regulator. This is also a popular set-up across Europe; for example, Fondation de France operates in a similar way and manages several hundred charitable donor-advised funds across France.

Community foundations

In the UK, there are strong networks of grant-makers that have a focus on supporting local grassroots charities and projects that aim to make an impact in a specific geographical area. Community foundations are a fabulous example of this. These are networks of grant-makers with the express aim of supporting and strengthening their own local communities. There are 47 community foundations at the time of writing, based across the length and breadth of the UK and giving out grants totalling almost £100 million a year between them.[17] While the sizes and scales of community foundations vary from one to another, they almost all manage funds that have been donated by people and organisations in their area, building on their endowment and providing a connection between local donors and local needs.

Livery companies

Similarly to community foundations, livery companies have a focus based upon their history within the City of London. There are 108 livery companies, including the large and well-known Goldsmiths, Merchant Taylors and Skinners, originally set up as guilds and regulators of their individual trades.[18] Many of the livery companies operate as grant-making charitable trusts today, usually supporting projects in and around London, although many also retain a regulatory role within their area of expertise. There are numerous, often historic and architecturally significant, livery company buildings across the City of London, and these are frequently used as venues for charity (and other) events.

Religious and church property funders

Other types of grant-maker include religious and church property funders, ranging from large trusts (such as Trust for London) to very small parochial funds. There are also those founded on property or land, such as the Henry Smith Charity, which was founded in 1628 and still includes large areas of Kensington among its assets.[19]

Private or family foundations

Over recent decades, there has been an explosion of personal philanthropy in the form of private or family foundations being set up by wealthy individuals as a means of charitable giving.[20] Not only can this be a very tax-effective way of managing philanthropic activity but it is also becoming more strategic, with many family foundations developing focused philanthropic interests and grant-making policies. Funders of this nature usually have a board of trustees predominantly made up of family members and may also bring in expertise on programme-specific giving – including employing professional staff – as they grow and develop their own strategy.

Corporate trusts and foundations

Trusts and foundations established by a corporate body are usually dependent on the profits of a company (or group of companies) in their ability to give out grants. Corporate grant-makers often start out as forms of CSR, and so their giving is likely to align with causes that are relevant to the company. The decision-makers in these types of grant-maker will usually be directors of the company or staff with a specific focus on CSR. Some corporate foundations grow, in both size and strategic grant-making, to become almost entirely independent entities. One example is Lloyds Bank Foundation, which has its own separate staff, trustees, policies and premises.

Institutional funders

Institutional funders are more distinct funding bodies, usually with a significant staff and often with their own funds derived from, or connected to, a public source (for example, the National Lottery Community Fund, formerly the Big Lottery Fund, or Comic Relief). Most institutional funders have great professional expertise among their staff base and many are also major policy influencers on a national or even global scale. Funding proposals for institutions like this are usually complex and focused on programmatic detail, with several rounds and deadlines, and the grants themselves are often large.

Although institutional funders (as well as statutory and European Union funders – see below) are formal and involve very specific criteria, they are still staffed by teams of people – with emotions, influences and connections – who engage directly with charities and make key funding decisions. Therefore, while this book is not specifically about these particular funder types, the processes we will explore remain very relevant to growing and maintaining these important relationships.

Statutory funding

This type of funding is available from government sources. In the UK, these include governmental departments, such as the Department for Education and the Foreign, Commonwealth and Development Office (known as FCDO and comprising the former Department for International Development (DfID)), from which charities may be eligible to receive funding for programmes deemed to fall under a governmental priority. The Channel Islands and separate country administrations (for example, the Welsh Parliament and Scottish Government) also have their own statutory funds available.

European Union funding

This is another significant income source for charities and, similarly to domestic statutory funding, often requires programmatic detail at numerous proposal stages. Fundraisers are required to work closely with programme teams to develop these types of proposal, which are made in response to the European Union's call for submissions relating to its numerous funding strands. For UK-based charities, leaving the European Union at the beginning of 2021 has brought into question how many of these strands will remain accessible going forward. Research from DSC has found that charities may face a collective loss of over £250 million should this valuable income source be entirely removed.[21]

Grant-making trends

An estimated total of £6.5 billion is given in grants to UK charities every year, from both private and public funders.[22] The top 300 philanthropic grant-makers make up over two-fifths (42%) of this amount. Of the other three-fifths, 29% comes from public or member-funded grant-makers, 18% focuses on only one single beneficiary or cause, and 11% comes from the National Lottery Community Fund.[23] Of all private giving in the UK, trusts and foundations make up 15.6% of charitable income and almost seven times the estimated direct giving by companies.[24]

Recipients of funding

Which organisations grant-makers fund depends upon their individual interests. However, collectively they have a strong reputation for supporting the full range of causes, including those deemed difficult to fund from other sources. In the 2020 *UK Civil Society Almanac* report, published by NCVO, international development organisations were found to have received the largest share of grants from grant-making voluntary organisations (38%), followed by religion-based charities (12%) and social services (12%).[25]

In the 2000s, the trend was for grant-makers to give increasingly strategically,[26] meaning that they gave for specific purposes and to fulfil particular objectives, and measured the impacts of their grants more rigorously. Some still gave general funding – unrestricted grants to be used as needed – but significant grants were usually restricted funds to be spent on particular projects. While this remains the case, there has at the same time been a resurgence among grant-makers in acknowledging the great value of unrestricted funding.[27] Major funders such as the Paul Hamlyn Foundation and the Esmée Fairbairn Foundation (in the UK) and the Ford Foundation (in the USA) have led the way in championing the giving of grants for general purposes. This kind of flexible funding is the holy grail for charities, as they are able to spend it exactly as needed, including on management costs such as staff salaries, IT equipment, office space rent and the many other expenses that are usually less attractive funding propositions but that are essential to continue running a charity from day to day. In many ways, this return to supporting core costs has become a redefined and welcome version of strategic grant-making, and was particularly recognised by funders (and valued by recipients) during the wake of the COVID-19 pandemic.

> We want to be a flexible and relational grant-maker. To achieve this, we work alongside the people and groups we fund to build open and trusting relationships – acknowledging their expertise and experience and drawing on their insights – to inform and develop the way we do things. The conversations that informed our refreshed strategy in 2020 and our experience of working with those we fund during the initial phase of the pandemic led us to rethink our main funding offer. Applicants can now tell us about the kind of support they need in the context of our priorities – from the underpinning or redesign of programmes, to supporting their core operations. We know that core funding gives charities the much-needed time and space to think, plan, try new approaches, and ensure financial security and flexibility. This way, organisations can get on with doing what they do best – and, when more organisations have that stability and headspace, the entire ecosystem benefits.
>
> Régis Cochefert, former Director of Grants and Programmes, Paul Hamlyn Foundation

Economic fluctuations

As grant-makers usually have their assets in investments and spend the dividends on their grant-making, their giving capacity can be subject to fluctuations in the economy. During times of economic uncertainty, such as following the financial crash in 2008, assets decline in line with the markets in which they are based. In the 2008–9 recession, UK foundations lost between 12.5% and 19% of their assets, compared with a 36% decline in the FTSE 100 stock market index. At the same time in the USA, the Dow Jones index saw a similar drop of 36% and US foundations lost an average of 20% of their asset values. However, amid these losses, UK foundations' giving declined by only between 2% and 9% and that of US foundations by only 2%: in both countries, grant-makers reduced their giving much less than their assets had declined.[28]

Both the UK and US grant-makers recovered their losses after the 2008–9 crash, but at a slower rate than the financial markets and generally less dramatically (in the USA, for example, foundations' investments increased by 58% from 2010 to 2018, but the Dow Jones grew by 140% over the same period).[29] It therefore seems that these funders experience less extreme shocks than other financial investments, but also have smaller peaks. These grant-makers also have a clear tendency to adjust their giving levels in response to times of crisis. A study by Candid found that 40% of the foundations it surveyed in the USA had adjusted their funding priorities during the 2008–9 recession.[30] Funders in the UK had a similar reaction: in 2020, ACF announced that 63% of its members had adjusted their giving in response to the COVID-19 pandemic.[31] Of these, some grant-makers set up wholly new funding streams (although these were mostly the community-focused foundations) and the majority made extra funding available for organisations working on their existing priorities.[32] Either way, funders on the whole tend to be resilient, reactive and supportive at times of particular need.

Competition for funding

Given this history of bolstering the charity sector, it is no surprise that income from grant-making bodies makes up a significant proportion of most charities' funding. Trusts and corporate fundraising typically make up over 10% of voluntary income[33] – and often an even higher proportion for smaller charities. Income from trusts and foundations is also consistently one of the most cost-effective forms of fundraising, with a return on investment (often referred to as ROI) of around 11:1 (around £11 in voluntary income received for every £1 invested in it);[34] additionally, it is the highest area of income growth across the various types of fundraising.[35] Charities often have high expectations when it comes to fundraising from trusts and foundations due to the potential size of grants and the range of core and project funding available, as well as the additional benefits of partnerships with grant-makers (such as added advocacy support and networks).

Given this reliance on grant-making as an important funding source, it is perhaps unsurprising that grant-makers have reported increases in both the numbers of applications received and the amount being asked for.[36] Fundraisers therefore need to be mindful of volume – the simple fact is that your proposal is likely to be one of many, possibly hundreds, to cross the desk of a funder in any given week. Grant-seekers also need to be aware that as grant-makers themselves vary, the type of decision-making that goes on behind the scenes is wide-ranging. Some trustees will meet at a kitchen table, others in a large board room. Some will have paid administrative staff to liaise with grantees and sift through applications received, while others will have applications drop through the letterbox of a trustee's house to be read by people who give their time voluntarily. This means the process of approaching grant-makers is complex and a one-size-fits-all approach will not get you far. Grants fundraising is both an art and a science: the art of understanding and nurturing a funder relationship and the science of crafting the proposal most likely to convince them of the worthiness of your cause.

A holistic view of grants fundraising

Traditionally, the skill of grants fundraising has focused heavily on the proposal-writing stage of the process. Some approaches will be made in person, in a meeting or other face-to-face context, but almost all significant funding requests will involve a written document that outlines the proposition to the funder – what exactly you are asking for and why. The content and quality of this written proposal are therefore paramount, and are likely to form the basis of a funder's decision.

However, this is only one piece of the puzzle. In order to secure the best, biggest and most sustainable funding partnerships, it is critical to look at the wider picture of the funder–charity relationship above and beyond the writing stage – or, more specifically, before and after. Everything up to the point of submitting a formal proposal is just as, if not sometimes more, important to achieving success as the proposal itself. And, indeed, everything that happens after you receive a grant will make a crucial difference in whether you receive further funding down the line and whether you are able to establish a long-lasting and fruitful partnership.

The approach cycle

The holistic view of grants fundraising looks at the entire relationship cycle – otherwise known as the approach cycle (or the solicitation cycle) –

as in figure 1.1. It gives precedence to the stages of research and planning, funder engagement and relationship-building, and the process of thanking and creatively stewarding the funder relationship either side of the written proposal itself.

FIGURE 1.1 The approach cycle

In fact, this cycle is relevant to all disciplines of fundraising; different terms may be used to describe each stage from one area to another, but essentially a donation of any size and type will go through some form of the approach cycle. When fundraising from grant-makers, there can be a tendency to overlook the first few stages, or perhaps to spend only a little time researching the funder and then go straight in with the written proposal. This is tempting, especially if there is an application deadline approaching faster than it seems possible to do much else, and even more so if there is internal pressure for funding to arrive yesterday. However, a longer-term perspective is important when seeking longevity from grant-maker partnerships; putting in the time at the earlier stages will most likely reap greater financial reward when a grant is finally forthcoming.

On the flip side, there is the danger of fundraisers spending so much time in the early stages, researching and trying to build connections and relationships with funders, that they rarely actually get around to submitting proposals, which in turn yields little income. Both of these approaches are problematic, and the smart fundraiser will seek to use their allotted time and resources as well as possible at each stage, as appropriate to the individual circumstances. We will look a little more at how to make these decisions as we go through the stages in turn.

The sponge cake model

Another way of considering how the approach cycle applies to grants fundraising is to use the more memorable analogy of a sponge cake: two thick sponge layers with a thinner jammy layer in the middle (a sandwich with a filling works equally well for those with a more savoury palate). The bottom sponge layer represents the initial four stages of the cycle (see figure 1.1), the middle jam layer represents the proposal itself and the top sponge layer represents the ongoing relationship management once a gift has been secured. The cake as a whole is built, layer by layer, from the bottom up (see figure 1.2).

FIGURE 1.2 The sponge cake model

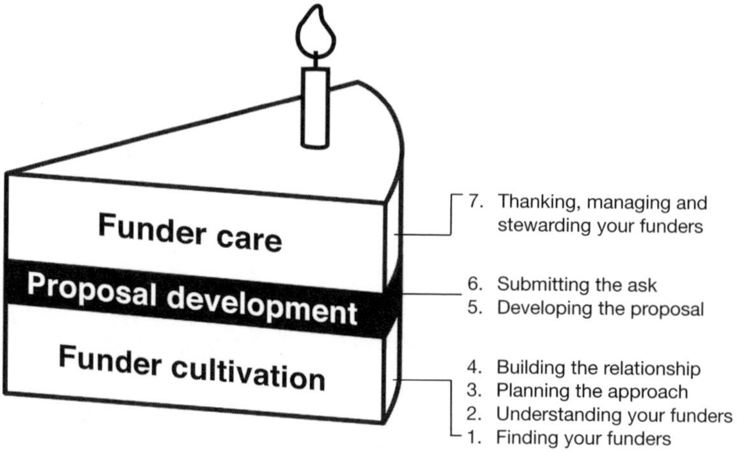

The crucial factor in this model is that time, resources and energy should be directed towards and equally prioritised between these outer layers, which are arguably the thicker substance of the cake (the funder relationship). The jam layer itself, while critically important, does not make a whole cake – or certainly not a very satisfying one.

Because of the importance of each of these seven stages, the chapters of this book focus on each stage in turn. You may find it helpful to dip into different chapters according to which phase you are currently in with a funder. It is also worth noting that if you have limited time or grants fundraising is only one aspect of your role, it may not be possible to implement everything that is explored at each stage. In those cases, it will be helpful to focus on the main take-away points, which are summarised at the end of each chapter. However, the overarching aim of this book is to make this point: great fundraising from grant-makers carefully considers all of these seven stages, and gives precedence to (and gets internal buy-in for) each and every one.

Spotlight: taking a holistic approach to grant-seeking

Just how important is a relationship-based approach to grant-seeking – does it really make that much of a difference?

A research report by Rogare, the fundraising think tank at Plymouth University's Centre for Sustainable Philanthropy, reviewed the concept of 'relationship fundraising' – a term coined by Ken Burnett in his influential book of the same name in 1992 (and used again in 2002 in the second edition).[37] Rogare undertook a year-long international review of the relationship-based approach, where fundraising focuses on the relationship between the funder and the charity as a means of maximising long-term income.[38]

The review suggests that whereas a shorter-term 'transactional' approach is effective and appropriate in mass-marketing fundraising, the relationship approach is applicable to high-value funders that have a greater level of involvement with the charity. Rogare also identified how current social psychology theories support the idea of relationship fundraising in fostering funders' commitment to, trust in and satisfaction with the organisations they support. Indeed, commitment, trust and satisfaction were found to be the key drivers of funder loyalty and lifetime value (i.e. cumulative giving to an organisation), and the report suggests that these three drivers are the most useful metrics for measuring success. The research also highlighted the need for charities' internal buy-in and support of this approach, to allow it to flourish.[39]

The charities Cancer Research UK and Changing Faces both find that focusing on the whole approach cycle – including conducting detailed funder research, seeking and cultivating relationships, and carefully considering their approach plan – is fundamental to their grants fundraising success:

> The members of the Philanthropy team at Cancer Research UK (CRUK) are first and foremost relationship managers; this is the cornerstone of what we do. Understanding at the outset of an approach what motivates trustees' support, and historical patterns of giving, alongside which areas of our work might be of interest is key to successful fundraising from trusts and foundations. I believe that fundraisers should focus on building and managing relationships, and therefore we work closely with specialists across prospect research, those who make decisions on the CRUK research investment and senior leadership in order to build a clear plan for each interaction, and in so doing, maximise the chances of successful cultivation.
>
> Susana Lopez, Head of Philanthropy, Cancer Research UK

> There's definitely more to a successful funding approach than just the proposal. At Changing Faces, we always aim to find out as much as we can, from publicly available information, about funders' interests, likely size of gift, and any relationships they might already have with our cause or people who are close to us, such as our trustees. That way, we can be sure to tailor our request to their priorities, ask for an appropriate amount, and make use of any connections which might add weight to the ask. It's important, however, to respect a funder's guidelines: if they state clearly that you need to follow a set application process, be prepared to do just that!
>
> Sue Canderton, Head of Philanthropy, Changing Faces

Conclusion

The world of grant-making is vast and diverse, and it enables incredible work to happen around the globe. While the charity landscape has continually evolved, this source of funding has remained true to its wonderfully rich history in its significant contribution to society. Successfully fundraising from grant-makers requires us to get to know them, looking beyond the proposal development part of the process and focusing on much more than just the 'jam' section of the sponge cake.

In a nutshell...

- Grant-making organisations usually exist solely to give money away. They make up a significant proportion of charitable income around the world, often supporting work that is otherwise difficult to fund.
- The types of grant-makers, and the terminology commonly used around them, vary greatly both within the UK funding landscape and in the wider global picture. Many grant-makers have a long history behind them and have frequently bolstered the charity sector during times of economic turmoil.
- The approach cycle, which gives equal importance to the activities before and after the written proposal, remains the same across the different funder types. It includes seven key stages for successful grant solicitation.
- The sponge cake model helps us to remember that funder cultivation is critical. This is followed by the proposal, which in turn is followed by the equally important funder care.
- A holistic view of grants fundraising is key to long-lasting, sustainable funding partnerships and will give you the edge over the competition.

Notes

1 Cathy Pharoah and Catherine Walker, *Foundation Giving Trends 2021* [PDF], Association of Charitable Foundations, 2021, www.acf.org.uk/common/Uploaded%20files/Research%20and%20resources/Research/Foundation%20Giving%20Trends/ACF179%20Foundation%20Giving%20Trends%202021_Design_DigitalVersion_v3.pdf, accessed 29 December 2021.

2 *Ibid.*, p. 5.

3 Harriet Whitehead, 'Number of new grantmaking trusts and foundations hit eight-year high in 2020' [web article], Civil Society, www.civilsociety.co.uk/news/number-of-grant-giving-foundations-and-trusts-established-is-highest-for-years.html, 1 February 2021.

4 Based on DSC's Funds Online (www.fundsonline.org.uk) data.

5 See, for example, HMRC's guidelines at www.gov.uk/government/publications/charities-detailed-guidance-notes.

6 Based on Merlin Waterson and Samantha Wyndham, *A History of the Barrow Cadbury Trust*, London, Barrow Cadbury Trust, 2013.

7 George Gleeson Bogert, 'Nathan Report and the Supervision and Enforcement of Charitable Trusts', *New York University Law Review*, vol. 29, 1954, p. 1078.

8 'About us' [web page], Association of Charitable Foundations, 2021, www.acf.org.uk/acf/About_us/ACF/About_Us/About_us.aspx?hkey=cbbdf44d-188d-4121-aebb-f3f476485f9c, accessed 7 December 2021.

9 *Giving USA 2021: The annual report on philanthropy for the year 2020*, Chicago, Giving USA Foundation, 2021.

10 'Our story' [web page], Bill and Melinda Gates Foundation, 2021, www.gatesfoundation.org/about/our-story, accessed 7 December 2021.

11 *Key Facts on U.S. Nonprofits and Foundations* [PDF], Candid, 2020, www.issuelab.org/resources/36381/36381.pdf, accessed 7 December 2021.

12 Paula D. Johnson, *Global Philanthropy Report: Perspectives on the global foundation sector* [PDF], Harvard Kennedy School and UBS, 2018, https://cpl.hks.harvard.edu/files/cpl/files/global_philanthropy_report_final_april_2018.pdf, accessed 7 December 2021.

13 Lawrence T. McGill, *Number of Registered Public Benefit Foundations in Europe Exceeds 147,000* [PDF], Foundation Centre, 2016, https://dafne-online.eu/wp-content/uploads/2019/08/pbf-report-2016-9-30-16.pdf, accessed 7 December 2021.

14 The reported number tends to fluctuate; see 'UK Civil Society Almanac 2019' [web page], NCVO, 2019, https://beta.ncvo.org.uk/documents/52/ncvo_uk_civil_society_almanac_2019_final.pdf, accessed 4 February 2022; 'UK Civil Society Almanac 2020' [web page], NCVO, 2020, https://ncvo-app-wagtail-mediaa721a567-uwkfinin077j.s3.amazonaws.com/documents/ncvo-uk-civil-society-almanac-2020.pdf, accessed 7 December 2021; and 'UK Civil Society Almanac 2021' [web page], NCVO, 2021, https://data.ncvo.org.uk, accessed 7 December 2021.

15 Cathy Pharoah and Catherine Walker, *Foundation Giving Trends 2021* [PDF], Association of Charitable Foundations, 2021, www.acf.org.uk/common/Uploaded%20files/Research%20and%20resources/Research/Foundation%20Giving%20Trends/ACF179%20Foundation%20Giving%20Trends%202021_Design_DigitalVersion_v3.pdf, p. 19, accessed 29 December 2021.

16 'UK Civil Society Almanac 2020' [web page], NCVO, 2020, https://ncvo-app-wagtail-mediaa721a567-uwkfinin077j.s3.amazonaws.com/documents/ncvo-uk-civil-society-almanac-2020.pdf, accessed 7 December 2021.
17 *UK Community Foundations: Report and financial statements for the year ended 31 March 2020* [PDF], UK Community Foundations, 2020, www.ukcommunityfoundations.org/media/ozgfeph4/ukcf-2020.pdf, accessed 7 December 2021.
18 *City Livery Companies* [PDF], City of London Public Relations Office, 2011, www.liverycommittee.org/wp-content/uploads/2020/06/City-Livery-Brochure.pdf, accessed 7 December 2021.
19 'History' [web page], The Henry Smith Charity, 2021, www.henrysmithcharity.org.uk/about-us/history, accessed 7 December 2021.
20 See 'The 10 biggest trends in family philanthropy' [web page], National Center for Family Philanthropy, 2015, www.ncfp.org/2015/11/23/the-10-biggest-trends-in-family-philanthropy, accessed 7 December 2021 and Paula D. Johnson, *Global Philanthropy Report: Perspectives on the global foundation sector* [PDF], Harvard Kennedy School and UBS, 2018, https://cpl.hks.harvard.edu/files/cpl/files/global_philanthropy_report_final_april_2018.pdf, accessed 7 December 2021.
21 Daniel Ferrell-Schweppenstedde, 'UK charities face Brexit funding cliff edge of more than £250m' [web article], Directory of Social Change, www.dsc.org.uk/content/uk-charities-brexit-funding-cliff-edge-250m, 21 November 2017.
22 Cathy Pharoah and Catherine Walker, *Foundation Giving Trends 2021* [PDF], Association of Charitable Foundations, 2021, www.acf.org.uk/common/Uploaded%20files/Research%20and%20resources/Research/Foundation%20Giving%20Trends/ACF179%20Foundation%20Giving%20Trends%202021_Design_DigitalVersion_v3.pdf, accessed 31 December 2021.
23 Cathy Pharoah and Catherine Walker, *Foundation Giving Trends 2019* [PDF], Association of Charitable Foundations, 2019, www.acf.org.uk/common/Uploaded%20files/Research%20and%20resources/Research/Foundation%20Giving%20Trends/ACF_Foundation_Giving_Trends_2019.pdf, accessed 31 December 2021.
24 Cathy Pharoah and Catherine Walker, *Foundation Giving Trends 2021* [PDF], Association of Charitable Foundations, 2021, www.acf.org.uk/common/Uploaded%20files/Research%20and%20resources/Research/Foundation%20Giving%20Trends/ACF179%20Foundation%20Giving%20Trends%202021_Design_DigitalVersion_v3.pdf, p. 5, accessed 31 December 2021.
25 'UK Civil Society Almanac 2020', [web page], NCVO, 2020, https://ncvo-app-wagtail-mediaa721a567-uwkfinin077j.s3.amazonaws.com/documents/ncvo-uk-civil-society-almanac-2020.pdf, accessed 7 December 2021.
26 John Kania, Mark Kramer and Patty Russell, *Strategic philanthropy for a complex world* [PDF], Stanford Social Innovation Review, 2014, www.oshkoshareacf.org/wp-content/uploads/2017/11/Strategic_Philanthropy_for_Complex_World-1.pdf, accessed 31 December 2021.
27 *Foundation Giving Trends Update 2020* [PDF], Association of Charitable Foundations, 2020, www.acf.org.uk/ACF/ACF/Research--resources/Research%20content/Research.aspx, accessed 7 December 2021.
28 Bill Bruty, *Keep Calm and Carry On... Giving* [PDF], Fundraising Training, 2020, www.fundraisingtraining.co.uk/s/Keep-Calm-and-Carry-On-November-2020.pdf, p. 3, accessed 7 December 2021.
29 *Ibid.*

30 Larry McGill, 'Foundations and the Great Recession: Context for our current crises' [web article], Candid, https://blog.candid.org/post/foundations-and-the-great-recession-context-for-our-current-crises, 30 March 2020.
31 'Covid-19: Results of ACF's survey on foundations' responses' [web article], Association of Charitable Foundations, www.acf.org.uk/acf/Newsfeed/2020/April-20/Covid-19-Results-of-ACFs-survey-on-foundations-responses.aspx, 15 April 2020.
32 Bill Bruty, *Keep Calm and Carry On… Giving* [PDF], Fundraising Training, 2020, www.fundraisingtraining.co.uk/s/Keep-Calm-and-Carry-On-November-2020.pdf, p. 5, accessed 7 December 2021.
33 'Fundratios 2014' [web page], Centre for Interfirm Comparison, 2014, www.cifc.co.uk/Fundratios14.html, accessed 7 December 2021.
34 *Unchartered Territory: Fundraising ROI's 2021* [PDF], LarkOwl, 2021, https://larkowl.uk/fundraising-benchmarking, accessed 31 December 2021.
35 'Fundratios 2014' [web page], Centre for Interfirm Comparison, 2014, www.cifc.co.uk/Fundratios14.html, accessed 7 December 2021.
36 *How Technology Will Transform the Charitable Sector for Fundraisers* [PDF], The Good Exchange, 2019, https://thegoodexchange.com/resources/technology-will-transform-charity-sector-fundraisers, p. 7, accessed 7 December 2021.
37 Ken Burnett, *Relationship Fundraising: A donor-based approach to the business of raising money*, San Francisco, Jossey-Bass, 2002.
38 Ian MacQuillin, *Relationship Fundraising: Where do we go from here? Volume 3 – Trends and challenges identified by practitioners* [PDF], Centre for Sustainable Philanthropy, Plymouth University, 2016, www.plymouth.ac.uk/uploads/production/document/path/11/11914/RF_-_Where_do_we_go_from_here_Vol_3.pdf, accessed 7 December 2021.
39 *Ibid.*

CHAPTER TWO

Finding your funders

Introduction

It is a common experience for fundraisers to have someone well-meaning come over, drop a copy of the Sunday Times Rich List[1] on their desk and say, 'Let's ask these folks for money!' While this might not be the most strategic way to go about it, what they are referring to is the hunt for prospects – the prospective funders who could potentially support your organisation's work.

Before you begin searching for prospects, it is essential to identify your specific funding needs. What do you need money for, when do you need it and how much do you need? This has to be worked out irrespective of what you think a grant-maker would *like* to support or what might sound like an attractive proposition. Once you are clear on these initial details, then you are ready to begin finding funders.[2]

It is worth noting that finding funders is the first stage of the approach cycle (see figure 1.1), rather than writing a proposal first and then looking for a funder to fit around it. The least ideal scenario is using a mail merge to fill in the name of the funder on a pre-written document and then just sending it off. Funders recognise these blanket mailings a mile off, and this approach tends to neither endear you to the recipient nor result in many grants. It is much more effective to develop a proposal for your specific funder from the outset. (Note that this is different from developing a project or programme for a specific funder – something we will look at in chapter 9; see page 150.)

There are two research stages – this initial prospecting stage and the more in-depth funder research stage, which we will explore in chapter 3. As such, chapter 3 is about understanding whom you are applying to, while this chapter is about finding them in the first place.

Identifying your prospects

> Prospect research is the fuel that powers the engine that is fundraising. It informs our approach at all points in the building of a relationship. It is also key to building our new business pipeline, which we seek to match based on our needs and the interests of potential partners. The appropriate fit, reputational alignment and ethical considerations are all informed by our prospecting.
>
> Jhumar Johnson, Chief of Staff to the Vice-Chancellor, The Open University

In theory, *all* funders are potential funders and therefore prospects. While most grant-makers have specific stated interests, it's not actually that uncommon for them to give a grant outside their usual remit. This might happen if one of the trustees has come across a particular project that has piqued their interest, been introduced to a charity that has especially caught their eye, or been approached through a personal connection. In such cases, they may be able to use their powers of discretion to direct funds to something the funder wouldn't normally support. In many ways, asking the question of whether there is an existing connection between your work and a funder is a useful starting point. Even if a link is not immediately obvious or you don't fit neatly into the funder's current priorities, the power of a connection can be very strong indeed.

That being said, with funders stating that 36% of the proposals they receive are ineligible[3] and with around 12,500 grant-makers in the UK alone,[4] how can we work out who our strongest prospects are? Very few of us have the time and resources to research every single possible funder in the hope of finding a way in. Indeed, a survey of UK grants fundraisers revealed that just over half (56%) felt they had identified most but not all prospective funders for their organisation, 41% felt there were more to find, and only 3% felt they had found them all.[5] It is helpful to have a system for finding the best prospects for a particular funding need and working out where to focus your attention. There are two main avenues to explore:

- **looking out:** finding funders that are completely new to your organisation;
- **looking in:** finding funders with an existing connection to you (but of whom you may be unaware).

Let's have a look at each of these in turn.

Looking out

'Prospecting' is the term used to describe the search for new funders (prospects). When undertaking prospecting, the most obvious place to start is to look for those with interests that align with your work – those with a clear fit. Almost all grant-makers have particular funding interests and these are usually publicly stated, which makes it much easier to determine a good fit compared to when you are fundraising from individuals. That said, bear in mind that we can find ourselves barking up the wrong tree if we misplace the focus of our search, as the following example illustrates.

The leaflets quandary

Let's imagine for a moment that you are working for a charity that supports elderly people in the local community. Your organisation does this by producing and distributing information leaflets about support services in the area. Your job as a fundraiser is to find the money to enable this important work, and you are looking for an organisation to fund your leaflets. A quick search online for grant-makers interested in funding leaflets doesn't turn up many, if any, fruitful results. What to do?

The simple solution is this: remember that no organisation will be looking to fund the *leaflets*. Rather, they will be looking to fund the *outcomes* for your beneficiary group (see page 93 for more detail on outcomes). In this case, the outcome would be the elderly people in your community being better supported through the new local services. Suddenly, there will be plenty of grant-makers that have the potential to support your work.

On the surface this might seem very obvious, but it is remarkably easy to forget when you first set out looking for prospects. We fall down at the first hurdle if we only search for funders with an interest in our activity rather than what we are looking to achieve as a result. Some grant-makers are very helpfully clear about what they do not fund in relation to specific activities. Common examples of funding exclusions include medical research, campaigning work, capital projects (such as buildings) and activities that are under the remit of government (therefore replacing statutory responsibility). Generally, however, it is what your activity will achieve – your impact – that is of real interest to a funder, and this is what should frame your search.

While a simple internet search may turn up some names, the most systematic way of finding new funders is to use some key research tools. These days there is a great range of services available to help you with this. Some of them require a subscription, but there are also lots of research tools at your disposal for free. Let's start with those:

Regulator registers

The website of the Charity Commission for England and Wales (CCEW) (https://register-of-charities.charitycommission.gov.uk) has an advanced search option that can bring up a list of funders with an interest in specific areas of charitable work. Note that all charities, both grant-making and grant-seeking, are registered with CCEW, so you will need to select the option 'Makes grants to organisations' or 'Makes grants to individuals' (as appropriate) to filter out those that are not funders. Most registered grant-makers will also have their accounts filed with CCEW, and it can be really useful to look at these to get a better idea of the kind of work and organisations they usually fund and at what level.

You can also get a sense of the financial trajectory of some grant-makers from looking at their filed accounts, such as any growth or depletion in their assets which may affect their funding levels. The Scottish Charity Regulator (OSCR) serves a similar function for grant-makers registered in Scotland (www.oscr.org.uk), as does the Charity Commission for Northern Ireland (CCNI) for funders based there (www.charitycommissionni.org.uk).

Funder reports

Grant-makers themselves often publish handy information in reports and many funders, particularly larger ones, include useful detail on their website. Both of these sources of information can help you to ascertain whether they are a good funding prospect. Remember that you are looking for top-level information at this point; more detailed research will come later. For now focus on their interests and the types of cause that they fund, the size of their grants, and any obvious connections to your organisation that stand out.

Fundraising networks

One of the best places to hear about new prospect opportunities is on the grapevine, which is easier to get on than you might think. There are numerous groups that discuss funding opportunities, and many of these groups are wonderfully open and collaborative places where grant-seekers meet up or talk online to share ideas and news about grant-makers – indeed, this openness is one of the great things about working in the charitable sector.

The UK's Chartered Institute of Fundraising has a special interest group (SIG) for each fundraising discipline, including a Trusts and Statutory SIG, a Researchers in Fundraising SIG and a Major Donor SIG, which are all worth exploring given their relevance to grant-makers.[6] The Trusts and Statutory SIG, at the time of writing, has a particularly active online forum with thousands of members who post questions and answers, information, and news about this area of funding. It can be a really great source for discovering new prospects via discussions, as well as gathering useful insight about them based on others' experiences. There are also regional SIGs as well as SIGs related to specific causes, such as Christian and cultural sector charities and a SIG for sole fundraisers working across a breadth of income streams. Social media also offers networking opportunities; the Trust Fundraising Hub, for example, is a Facebook group run by Money Tree Fundraising and also has an active and very helpful discussion forum.[7]

Competitors

Another useful place to look is at the annual reports of charities similar to yours: your grant-seeking competitors. Most fundraising charities publish their annual report on their website and there is often a list of supporters, including grant-making trusts and foundations, somewhere within the report (often at the back). A good leaf through the report itself may give you more insight into what some grant-makers have specifically funded, so look out for any highlighted projects that mention funder names. In the UK, all charities are required to submit their accounts to CCEW (in England and Wales), CCNI (Northern Ireland) or OSCR (in Scotland) if their total income is over a certain threshold, so if you can't find an annual report, have a look at your competitor charities' accounts to see whether you can identify any clues.

Also get into the habit of keeping an eye out for funder acknowledgements in general – once you start looking out for them, you'll spot lists of funders in the entrance halls to many buildings (such as museums, galleries, educational institutions, hospitals and hospices). Take a photo when you spot one or make a note of any funder names you've never heard of before, and do some quick research when you next have a chance to see whether the organisation could be a prospect for your work too.

Free online databases

There are some websites that provide lists of potential funders for free, such as the Charity Excellence Framework (www.charityexcellence.co.uk), which has a 'Funding Finder' database and links to other grant funding databases and online lists. Get Grants (www.getgrants.org.uk) also provides information about grant-makers with interests in particular areas of work across the sector.

Paid-for resources

If you have the budget, subscription or paid-for prospecting resources are well worth the investment and can provide you with a strong list of funder names. Some of these enable access to databases which contain detailed information about funders and are regularly updated, while others provide catalogues of new grant-making opportunities to leaf through:

- **Funds Online** (www.fundsonline.org.uk) was created and is run by the Directory of Social Change (DSC). It offers a flexible subscription service through which you can access a detailed directory of over 8,000 grant-making sources, including trusts and foundations, companies, and statutory funders. Hard-copy directories are also published by DSC and include *The Guide to Major Trusts*, *The Directory of Grant Making Trusts* and *The Guide to New Trusts* (also available as a download). The guides provide details of UK grant-makers' priorities and funding activities and can be purchased at www.dsc.org.uk/publications.

- **My Funding Central** (www.myfundingcentral.co.uk) is a regularly updated database of thousands of UK funding sources including charitable trusts, societies and local authorities. The service is free for small charities with an annual income under £30,000 and available by annual subscription for organisations with a higher turnover.
- **GrantFinder** (www.grantfinder.co.uk) is a database covering local, national and international sources of funding. GrantFinder provides a lot of detail on each grant-maker it features, although the subscription cost is high.
- **GrantsOnline** (www.grantsonline.org.uk) is a daily updated searchable database of grants opportunities from the European Union, UK government agencies, lotteries, and grant-making trusts and foundations.
- **Factary** (www.factary.com) provides the New Trust Update service, which is a detailed summary of newly registered grant-makers, as well as access to its back catalogues of existing grant-maker profiles.
- **NewCharities** (www.newcharities.org) provides a monthly Trust List on a subscription basis, containing a summary of every grant-making organisation newly registered with CCEW.
- **Invisible Grantmakers** (www.socialpartnershipmarketing.co.uk) is an annually produced report that identifies and profiles lesser-known grant-makers that are not featured in the more widely published and online directories.

There are also several sources relevant outside the UK:

- **Candid** (https://fconline.foundationcenter.org) provides a directory of US-based foundations which is accessible with a subscription.
- **FoundationSearch** (www.foundationsearch.com) offers a database of over 140,000 US and Canadian foundations through its subscription service.
- **Philea – Philanthropy Europe Association** (https://philea.issuelab.org) has a similar resource with an online library of information about foundations and funding opportunities based in Europe.
- **Europa International Foundation Directory** (www.routledge.com/The-Europa-International-Foundation-Directory/book-series/EIFD) provides an annual and comprehensive directory of global grant-makers, although it is an expensive publication.

The list of sources given above is not exhaustive and new prospecting services are cropping up all the time, but these are the classic tried-and-tested resources to consider. Remember that the cost of even one or two of these services may result in funding that pays for itself many times over: speculate to accumulate, as they say. Many online prospecting tools also include the option of setting up alerts so that you are emailed when new funding opportunities become available for your specific area of work. These are really useful to save you regularly trawling through websites. It may be worth having a separate email folder to pop the alerts in to look through at a set time and save your inbox from being overwhelmed with notifications.

Other options

If you have limited capacity or don't have a prospect research specialist within your organisation, there is also the option of hiring a prospect research consultant or an agency which can look at your current prospect list and identify potential additional funders. If budgets don't allow for outsourcing support, the tools mentioned in this section should certainly give you a strong start in developing your prospect pool. Blocking out an hour in your calendar once a week is worthwhile to keep prospecting at the forefront and not have it slip down a list of other priorities.

Looking in

The old adage goes that 80% of your funding is likely to come from 20% of your funders – in high-value fundraising areas such as grants income, it may even be more like 90% from 10% for some charities. Furthermore, grant-seeking organisations usually find that their existing funder pool makes up the lion's share of their annual grants income. Some of your best prospects, therefore, need not be names that are brand new to you. In fact, some of your strongest prospects will be those that have had contact with you in the past or, even better, given grants to your organisation previously but at a lower level or several years ago. Almost a third (32%) of UK charities are yet to research the grant-makers that have supported them before but are no longer current funders (known as 'lapsed funders') to see whether they might be able to reapply.[8] These funders provide a ripe opportunity to be reignited (in the case of lapsed funders) or uplifted (in the case of current funders).

Reigniting lapsed funders and uplifting current funders

Lapsed funders are a fantastic and often overlooked prospect source, since their previous giving indicates an affinity with the potential to be reignited. Successfully re-engaging with such funders requires some analysis and research, both to uncover their presence and to explore why they stopped giving. It could be that their priorities and interests changed, or that you were precluded from further funding for a while as a condition of the previous grant, or perhaps the relationship simply went stale and they were just not asked again. Whatever the reason, spending time unearthing lost previous donors is well worth the effort.

It can be useful to categorise lapsed donors into three groups: recently lapsed (those that have given within the past two to five years), very lapsed (given five to ten years ago) and extremely lapsed (given over ten years ago). You can then take a different approach to each group accordingly, noting that the more lapsed the funder, the colder the relationship is likely to be and the greater the chance that there has been a turnover of key contacts since. The extremely lapsed group should be treated as new prospects, since the relationship will need to be re-established and it is likely that both you and the funder will have new staff, projects and priorities to rediscover. We will return to these three groups in chapter 4 (see page 63) when we take a look at how to plan your approach.

While they are not strictly prospects, it is also important to look at your current funders and always be asking whether you could uplift (i.e. increase) their giving. Grant-makers frequently have lists of the type of funding they give on a regular basis, such as a small grants list for the annual funds they distribute at the lower end of their giving. It could be that you have been on a small grants list for a number of years, but actually the grant-maker has the capacity to be funding your organisation on a much larger level if the project is the right fit and the relationship can be nurtured appropriately. We will look at how to do this in more detail in chapter 5.

Carrying out an internal audit

An internal audit is a handy way to explore the potential from these funder groups. Whether you're using a database or a simple spreadsheet, this will give you a sense of who your current, previous and completely new (prospective) funders are and their potential going forward.

As much as possible, run a list of all grant-makers on your database (however complex or simple it may be) and sort the data to glean the following information:

- **Which funders have supported you in the past one, two to five, five to ten, and more than ten years?** Sorting by last gift will help you to find these groups. These will become your 'current', 'recently lapsed', 'very lapsed' and 'extremely lapsed' groups. You will then be able to tailor your approaches accordingly.
- **Which funders are on your database but, for whatever reason, have never given a grant?** These will go onto your prospects list. Are there any here with good potential, if you can re-establish the relationship?

- **Which funders have been your biggest to date, including single and cumulative grants?** This can help to tease out any current or previous funders that may appear to be small grant-makers but actually have a high long-term value to your organisation and could benefit from greater stewardship (we will look at this more in chapter 8) to maintain or uplift their support.
- **Which funders have given to you year on year, or very regularly, and are your most loyal supporters?** These grant-makers are most likely to have you on their regular giving list. It's worth checking that the regular gifts you are getting are at the best potential level, rather than assuming you are receiving the maximum in potential grants.

The answers to these questions should give you a picture of the funders with which you have already had some form of engagement. You can then categorise them in a helpful way to inform the approach you take.

If you have a large fundraising department, do also check for grant-makers that are currently under a different team, such as direct marketing, regional fundraising or corporate fundraising. Small trusts, in particular, can often get lost in direct marketing systems and receive mailings better designed for individual givers. These funders may be better pulled out and managed more appropriately as small grant-makers. Small trusts may also wind up at some point and make significant one-off gifts before they close down, *if* the relationship has been managed well. (Chapter 9 looks at how to manage large numbers of small trusts; see page 152.) Similarly, for larger charities with regional offices, some regional grant-maker relationships may be held by regionally based staff. In this case it is essential that the knowledge of who is holding which relationships is shared and that all correspondence, planning and any potential funder links are co-ordinated.

Exploring your networks: a peer review

One of the best paths to finding funders is using and expanding your networks. Your trustee board, your staff and even your current donors may have helpful untapped connections and be able to link you with a prospect. These are known as peer-to-peer connections. For some charities it may feel like these networks are few or non-existent, but it just takes one good connector to be willing to make links on your behalf for a good and growing peer-led network to emerge.

Undertaking a peer review is a great way to unearth and explore these links. A peer review is a simple exercise whereby a list of prospects (and/or lapsed or potential-to-uplift funders) is given to someone who then notes down which funders they know and identifies their ability and willingness to connect you. Done well, it can also help to spark ideas about other potential funders that are not already on your list. Presenting a list for peer review is likely to be more successful than just asking, 'Hi, do you know any funders?' and you are more likely to elicit further suggested names and contacts in the process.

Trustee and development board members, fundraising committee members, senior staff, patrons and high-level volunteers, and even potential suppliers (such as companies with likely connections) and beneficiaries (such as high-profile or well-connected alumni) can all be great people with whom to conduct a peer review. Current funders that you have very warm relationships with may also be willing to undertake the exercise. Tailoring the peer review document to the person you are presenting it to will give you the best chance of unearthing funder links, such as by their particular industry (for example, media, technology or finance) or location (for example, the city or county where they live or conduct business).

You can present the peer review as a table, where the person simply ticks the boxes according to their level of connection and ability to facilitate links with potential funders. Include the names of any key people – such as a grant-maker's trustees, directors or other key decision-makers – to whom you would like to find a link. Your document might look something like table 2.1.

TABLE 2.1 Example peer review exercise template

Name	**Know very well** (e.g. close contact)	**Know quite well** (e.g. social or business associate)	**Know a little** (e.g. socially connected enough to say 'hello')	**Do not know**	**Able to write to or contact**	**Notes**
The Pretend Charitable Trust *Trustees:* *Mr Ahmed A., Dr Belinda B., Mr Christopher C.*						
Made Up Foundation *Director: Mrs Maria Smith* *Trustees:* *Mr Ray XYX, Mrs Safiya XYZ*						
The Fictional Fund *Trustees:* *Mr Joe Bloggs, Mrs Julie Bloggs*						

The reason for including the four levels of closeness (from 'Know very well' to 'Know quite well' to 'Know a little' to 'Do not know') is to encourage the person to really think about the depth of the connection and how comfortable they are in making an introduction on your behalf. Of course, you can adapt the table as needed, but keep it simple – it needs to feel quick and non-arduous for the person filling it out. Around 30 funder names per list is probably enough so as not to be overwhelming, but do leave some spaces at the bottom for any extras the person may think of and a column for notes to capture any nuggets of information or useful insights.

The 'Able to write to or contact' box is important: just because someone is connected to a funder, it doesn't mean they will feel comfortable or able to make direct contact themselves. There may still be value in the connection if they are able to give you any additional information about the funder, to inform your research and approach planning. Conversely, someone may not know a funder but still be willing to make contact on your behalf by way of an introduction – depending on who they are, this can still be very helpful and we will look at this more in chapter 4 (see page 63).

Aim to conduct a peer review annually to keep your search for connections fresh. Doing it regularly also keeps prospecting front of mind for your potential connectors and reminds them to come to you when they think of or make a new useful peer link. You could even make a peer review a standing item at your trustees' board meeting or annual general meeting – perhaps during a coffee break for individual trustees to fill out, or as a more formal agenda item if it's the kind of group where a bit of competitive brainstorming might fuel ideas. It is also important to reassure anyone filling out a peer review form that you'll manage their contacts carefully and tactfully (see 'A note on data protection' on page 47) and that you will keep them updated on progress.

Once you have the document back, let the person know that you or someone from your team will be in touch to follow up. You can then glean more information about any identified connections at that later stage, rather than asking the person to note everything down all at once (which could be quite time-consuming if they know a lot of people). If you are with them at the time and they are very chatty while filling the form out, it might be worth having a separate copy yourself to write in the notes section and capture anything useful they share. At other times it could work best to give the form to someone to take away and fill out on their own, when they have more time to think about it. Use your judgement about what feels most appropriate. Of course, make sure you spell all the names correctly and that the information you include is accurate and up to date.

Note that a peer review doesn't always have to be a formal exercise with a long list of names. If you have identified a single grant-maker that looks like a good potential fit, you can ask your contacts the same questions about the one funder to look for a connection. Getting into this connections-seeking mindset generally is very valuable – whether you use a formal peer review (as in table 2.1) or just phone or email around to ask, always aim to find a link before you move into preparing your approach and written proposal. It is also important to note that if you use peer-to-peer processes like this, you will need to say so in your organisation's privacy notice for data protection purposes, which is covered in more detail in the next chapter (see page 48).

Qualifying your prospects

Once you have done your internal and external research and have a good list of prospects, the next step is to shortlist them to help you prioritise which to focus on first. An exercise called qualification is a really useful way of doing this. Qualifying your prospects involves giving ratings to prospective funders based on two main criteria: their capacity and propensity to give a grant to your organisation.

Capacity

Capacity looks at how much a grant-maker has to give, including the typical size or range of grants, and the potential trajectory of grant-making over time (for example, a growth in the funder's assets might indicate the potential for larger grants, and any investment losses could indicate the grant-maker is likely to scale back subsequent grant-making). Capacity also considers funders' longer-term capacity for support, including multi-year grants and possible patterns of grant-making, such as giving one-off grants versus giving year-on-year support. A good delve into a grant-maker's annual accounts can reveal some of this information; you should look particularly closely at grantee lists and the top-level financial information pages.

Propensity

Propensity looks at the likelihood of a funder making a grant to your charity. It considers the amount of overlap between your and the funder's programmatic interests, the level of personal connection you have, and the likely motivation for the decision-makers to choose your organisation over other applicants. The importance of propensity cannot be overstated. It is easy to do some quick research focusing mostly on capacity and then to write off a funder as a prospect because there don't seem to be big grants given to causes like yours. Propensity is actually the more important factor, as, given enough interest in and connection with your cause, funders can decide to commit to larger grants than might be obvious from a cursory look at capacity alone. You also may not always know whether they are looking to spend out their funds or wind down, or are expecting an injection of assets which might change their grant-making capacity over time.

It is worth noting that funders that support causes similar to yours may not necessarily score highly on propensity as a prospect. This is because funders that are giving year on year to a similar cause may feel they are already fulfilling that part of their grant-making through the other organisation, or have a level of commitment to your 'competitor'. On the other hand, if you are doing a different activity in the same area (for example, you work at ground level and the competitor works at policy level), a funder may consider it complementary to support you both. If the funding to the other organisation appears to be sporadic, rather than long term, this may also be a positive indication of the funder's propensity to consider your work in addition, or instead.

Using capacity and propensity to rate your prospects

Allocating rating numbers to capacity and propensity indicators is very much an intuitive exercise: you will need to use your best judgement based on the information you have. Remember that they are just that – indicators – and not hard-and-fast rules about who is going to give you the best grants.

Table 2.2 offers an example of a basic qualification model, which can be adapted. For example, you may want to amend the 'Likely single grant capacity' row to what would constitute a small, medium or large grant for your organisation. Simply enter scores (0–3) in the final column for each category under both capacity and propensity and then add up all the scores to get an overall total. Do this for each prospect you have. The prospects with the highest overall totals will be your strongest and those you should prioritise.

TABLE 2.2 Example prospect qualification table

	0	1	2	3	Score
Capacity					
Likely single grant capacity	Less than £5,000	£5,000–£10,000	£10,000–£50,000	More than £50,000	
Longevity of support	Grant-making appears to be decreasing	Grant-making appears to be increasing, or there appears to be growth in assets	Gives over multiple years as well as one-off grants	Gives long-term support to organisations (e.g. year-on-year grants)	

	0	1	2	3	Score
Propensity					
Fit with stated programmatic interests and activities	No or little fit	Some fit, or some grants given to similar causes	Good fit, or several grants given to similar causes	Strong fit, or large/frequent grants given to similar causes	
Level of connection to our organisation	No known connection	Some connection (e.g. distant peer-to-peer link)	Good connection (e.g. close peer-to-peer link)	Strong connection (e.g. very close peer-to-peer link)	
Key decision-makers' experience of our cause	No known experience of our cause or organisation	Some experience of our cause or organisation	Good level of experience of our organisation (e.g. staff link)	Strong experience (e.g. personal/ family beneficiary or previous staff)	
				Total:	

Note that the size of your shortlist, or the number of prospects you choose to prioritise for the next stage, will depend on your role and the resources available to you. If grants fundraising is only part of your role, you may initially need to choose the top ten or so to make best use of your time. If your role is specific to grants fundraising, you may choose to move all of those with a rating over 8 (for example) into your portfolio to take to the next stage. Don't lose the lower-scoring prospects altogether, though. Keep them on file to review again in six or so months' time.

The qualification process has benefits in addition to identifying your top prospects. It also highlights whether there are any crucial gaps in your information. For example, if you are not yet clear on a grant-maker's capacity, you will need to go back and do some more digging before progressing with your funder approach. Furthermore, it provides a useful justification for your data protection processes at the next research stage, which we will examine in chapter 3 (see page 47).

Spotlight: the five pathways to funders

In 2017 Bill Bruty, founder and director of Fundraising Training Ltd, began a piece of research to explore the routes through which charities find and initiate relationships with grant-makers. Over the course of four years, Bruty conducted interviews with over 600 recipients of major gifts – across different sizes and types of cause – in the UK, Africa and the USA. The main question asked of the charities was: 'How did your funder relationship start?'

From this analysis, there were five clear pathways:

- **unsolicited grants**, initiated seemingly out of the blue by the funder;
- **uplifted grants**, from funders that had given to the charity before but at a much lower level;
- **peer-endorsed grants**, from funders that had been introduced to the charity by another party;
- grants from funders that had a **strong experience or existing connection** to the charity, such as a previous employee, or a family member or friend of a beneficiary;
- **proactively solicited grants**, where the charity fully initiated the contact and proposal process.

While all the received grants likely involved a proposal to the funder at some stage in the process, they could all be attributed to one of these pathways. Notably, only the fifth pathway involves sole proactive solicitation by the charity – the other four pathways all involve the funder initiating the relationship in some other way.

These findings have significant implications for grant-seeking fundraisers. They show us that by only focusing on finding new funders that we can instantly approach, we are missing a huge number of potential relationship opportunities. The value of prospect research at the initial stage – exploring both internal and external connections – is paramount to securing income across all the pathways.

The first pathway is particularly interesting, as on the surface it may appear that there is little a charity can do to achieve more unsolicited gifts. In fact, this is not quite true. Funders that give seemingly out of the blue have to know about you first. Many funders are proactive in their approach to grant-making and will be actively looking for charities with interesting work that aligns with their objectives. Fundraisers need to be aware of this and working with others in their wider organisation to ensure that projects, case studies and funding needs have a strong platform, using tools such as websites, social media and a presence at relevant sector events. Simply put, not only do we need to be finding funders but we also need to make sure we can be easily found by them.

Conclusion

Once you are clear what your funding needs are, identifying who could support your work is the very first stage in the approach cycle (see figure 1.1). This initial research will not only give you a list of funders to approach but also form the first step in establishing the information you will need to put together the best possible proposal.

In a nutshell…

- Finding new funders is known as prospecting. It will take time and effort, but it does not need to cost a lot given the growing range of prospect research tools available.
- Prospecting involves looking out for new funding opportunities as well as looking at your existing networks and links, and the unlocked potential of lapsed funders.
- Conducting a peer review – exploring a list of prospects with potential connectors – is a great way to unearth hidden links and to use the influence of those in your networks to help you reach prospective funders.
- Qualifying your prospects is a ranking exercise that helps to prioritise your funder shortlist and work out where best to focus your energies, as well as where you need to do more research.
- The majority of charities' grants do not come from submitting a cold proposal; most involve more complicated engagement and interaction to initiate a relationship, including maximising the chances of funders proactively finding you.

Notes

1 'The Sunday Times Rich List 2021' [web page], *The Times*, 2021, www.thetimes.co.uk/sunday-times-rich-list, accessed 7 December 2021.

2 Another title in this series – *Fundraising Strategy* – is a helpful resource for considering these broader fundraising questions (see Claire Routley and Richard Sved, *Fundraising Strategy*, London, Directory of Social Change, 2021).

3 *Ineligible Applications: The wasted work of the voluntary sector* [PDF], Directory of Social Change, 2010, www.dsc.org.uk/wp-content/uploads/2015/09/IneligibleApplicationsfinal.pdf, accessed 7 December 2021.

4 The reported number tends to fluctuate; see 'UK Civil Society Almanac 2019' [web page], NCVO, 2019, https://beta.ncvo.org.uk/documents/52/ncvo_uk_civil_society_almanac_2019_final.pdf, accessed 4 February 2022; 'UK Civil Society Almanac 2020' [web page], NCVO, 2020, https://ncvo-app-wagtail-mediaa721a567-uwkfinin077j.s3.amazonaws.com/documents/ncvo-uk-civil-society-almanac-2020.pdf, accessed 7 December 2021; and 'UK Civil Society Almanac 2021' [web page], NCVO, 2021, https://data.ncvo.org.uk, accessed 7 December 2021.

5 *Funding Social Change: How can grant-seekers and grant-makers collaborate to better serve our communities?* [PDF], KEDA Consulting, 2021, www.kedaconsulting.co.uk/wp-content/uploads/2021/06/keda_consulting_funding_social_change_a4_50pp_V2.pdf, p. 17, accessed 7 December 2021.

6 See 'Regional and special groups' [web page], Chartered Institute of Fundraising, https://ciof.org.uk/about-us/groups, accessed 4 February 2022.

7 See 'Trust Fundraising Hub' [web page], Facebook, www.facebook.com/groups/trustfundraisinghub, accessed 4 February 2022.

8 *Funding Social Change: How can grant-seekers and grant-makers collaborate to better serve our communities?* [PDF], KEDA Consulting, 2021, www.kedaconsulting.co.uk/wp-content/uploads/2021/06/keda_consulting_funding_social_change_a4_50pp_V2.pdf, p. 17, accessed 7 December 2021.

CHAPTER THREE

Understanding your funders

Introduction

Imagine that you're baking a cake and you have a bunch of ingredients laid out but no recipe. You know it will probably involve some eggs, some flour, maybe a bit of sugar at some point... but how much of each and in what order? Are you missing some other essential ingredients? And even once you've got it all mixed together, what temperature should you bake it at? This is where funder research comes in. Research provides the recipe for your approach: it tells you what ingredients are needed and how to put them together to produce the best possible result.

Good funder research will shape everything from how you make first contact and engage with a funder to the style in which you write the proposal document itself. It will also provide you with extremely useful insight for when it comes to thanking and stewarding a funder upon receipt of a grant. So don't go jumping straight in with writing your proposal just yet – step away from that pen! – because this research stage is your best bet for funding success.

Whether you're looking at new, lapsed or current funders for your organisation, your research will inform (or update) your understanding of how to:

- approach the funder;
- create the proposal;
- manage the relationship, whether successful or not.

You can potentially end up on a bit of a wild goose chase once you start your research, but keeping these three things front of mind will prevent you from meandering too far from your purpose. If you find your research is no longer addressing at least one of these points, then you know it's time to move on.

What to look for

It's likely that you've already learned a lot of useful information about your potential funder from the initial prospecting stage, so you may already have a good sense of what your prospect's grant capacity, previous grant recipients and main priorities are. You now need to dig deeper and fill in any gaps in this knowledge.

> Doing your research shows that you're invested in achieving a positive outcome. This means preparing as well as you can by researching funders to understand how they like to work with others, and thinking through all the partnership options to make the proposal as compelling, unique and relevant as possible.
>
> Holly Hastings-Payne, Head of Philanthropy, Macmillan Cancer Support

Specifically, you need to discover the *who*, *what*, *why* and *how*. Each one is covered in the following sections.

The who

A commonly used phrase in fundraising is 'people give to people'. It's said a lot for a good reason: because it's true! We may intrinsically know this – that people are most influenced by other people, rather than objects or abstract ideas, and it's other humans that are most likely to capture our hearts and minds in some way to inspire us to act.[1] In grants fundraising, we talk a lot about grant-makers as organisations and institutions, which can make them seem quite faceless. However, even the most complex statutory funder is run, organised and directed by human beings. It is therefore hugely helpful to find out who these key individuals are and what their motivations and influences may be.

Key research questions you can use to understand the people behind a funder are:

- **Who are the main decision-makers – that is, whom do you need to convince?** They may be trustees, a panel or board of directors, a group of family members, or others overseeing funds, such as a solicitor. You might also need to convince a combination of these groups.

- **Are there any gatekeepers or key staff?** Many, especially larger, grant-makers have professional staff such as grant managers and administrative personnel, often known as gatekeepers, who may do an initial sift of proposals received. This makes them hugely influential, as it is their decision whether or not your proposal even reaches the sight of the final decision-makers.

- **Are there any advisers you should know about?** Some funders hire consultants who can help applicants with their proposal at the initial draft stage or may have influence over grant-making decisions. Advisers might also include solicitors or accountants who are not personally associated with the grant-maker but may still make key decisions and/or have great influence over how funds are directed.

- **Are you or your organisation linked to anyone at the grant-maker?** If you carried out a peer review exercise (see page 28), you may have already identified some helpful connections. Otherwise, look for any overlap with key individuals in terms of their education, industry, location, social interests and networks, as well as whether they are on the boards of any other grant-makers. If so, who are the other trustees of *those* organisations – whom will they therefore know?

• **Are there any relationship clues?** As well as factual information about who's who and who knows whom, try to unearth any hints about building a person-to-person relationship with the funder. Perhaps a media article will uncover that a key trustee has attended events at other charities, indicating that they might accept an invitation to something, or perhaps you'll discover that you have a shared interest in something that could be useful to bring up in conversation.

> I once discovered that the chair of a prospective funder was from the same town as my charity's CEO. This became a handy nugget of information when I introduced them to each other later on at a charity event. It initiated a warm conversation which then led on to other matters.
>
> **Trust fundraiser**

The what

Hopefully, you will already have an idea about what your prospective grant-maker likes to fund, from your initial prospect research. And, if you've reached this point, it's likely that there's some obvious alignment between your work and the funder's priorities. Now is the time to look much more closely at grant-making patterns, to inform exactly what you ask for and for how much.

Key research questions you can use to understand what a funder supports are:

• **What is the usual grant range?** A grant of £500 will be large for some funders and very small for others. Others again may give a whole range of grants, from small to very large, and have specified grants programmes at various funding levels. Look particularly at the level of grants usually given to organisations and projects similar to yours.

• **What is the usual grant type?** Some grant-makers prefer to give one-off grants, others prefer making multi-year commitments and still others prefer a mix of the two. If there is the potential for a large grant from a particular funder, consider whether asking for this over multiple years might be more likely to be successful (if it fits with your project's needs) or whether the funder seems more likely to distribute large grants in one go. Some funders also prefer to give 'hatcher grants': giving early into a project's fundraising, so that their grant can be used to attract other funding. Others prefer to give 'finisher grants': only giving once they are confident that a project's funding target will be met.

- **What are the grant-maker's stated project interests and does its actual grant-making reflect them?** Delve into the specifics of what the funder does and explicitly does not fund; some funders have very narrow and defined criteria and others are more open to interpretation. Look for any clues in reports and media articles for details of what the funder usually supports – for example, is it mainly capital projects (such as buildings and equipment), salaries for specific roles, or core costs? Furthermore, a look at which organisations the funder has actually awarded grants to over the years (you will be able to find this information in the grant-maker's published accounts) may shed light on any discrepancies between the stated preferences and the projects actually funded. For example, if you notice a grant award to a charity or project that doesn't seem to fit among the grant-maker's usual grantees list, it may well be that there is more flexibility than is initially apparent, which could perhaps be unlocked with the right connection.

- **What kinds of organisation has the grant-maker funded in the past?** Some sectors may be more favoured than others, even if the grant-maker states a broad interest in charitable activities. Look for any sector preferences or recurrent themes, such as most grants going towards the arts, or whether there is an equal spread across the funder's interests. Similarly, check back through a few years' worth of accounts to see whether the funder tends to support the same causes year on year (and at the same levels every year) or whether there are regularly new grantees; this will give you an indication of your chances if you are a new applicant.

- **What is the current grant-making trajectory?** Some funders have pretty stable grant-making levels year on year, while others spend more on larger grants some years and less in others, so look for any patterns in the financials. If there has been a growth in assets, for example, there may be more money to give out in the following years. Or a grant-maker may be 'spending out' – i.e. giving more and more in grants as its capital begins to decrease. Being able to detect these patterns will help you to spot where there are ripe opportunities.

The why

Intrinsically linked with the *who* and the *what* is the question of *why* grant-makers do what they do. Grant-makers exist to give money away, but getting underneath the reasons for their particular funding activities can be extremely useful in shaping your approach.

Key research questions you can use to understand a funder's motivations are:

- **Why was the grant-maker originally set up?** Search for any information or clues about the history of the organisation, including who established it and what the initial aims and objectives were. Perhaps there is a historical link with the current grant-making priorities and the original founder's vision, for example.

- **What are the grant-maker's core values and beliefs?** A family trust may be founded upon a sense of altruism, for instance, perhaps motivated by wanting to give back or fulfil a sense of moral or religious obligation. Less altruistically, you may be dealing with more of a tax-efficiency vehicle than a philanthropy-based enterprise. A corporate foundation might be driven primarily by business growth, with the wider aim being to promote a positive public perception of the company or to inspire its staff. Look for the underlying principles behind a funder's motivations.

- **Why does the grant-maker seem to support its current grantees?** Some grant-makers choose to focus on supporting smaller charities, for example if they feel that their role is to fill the gaps, while others tend to support larger, well-known causes, perhaps based on their reputation in a given field. Other funders might feel a strong pull to support local charities working with beneficiaries in their geographical area. Yet others may have historical or personal connections, for example by giving grants to educational institutions previously attended by trustees.

- **Is the grant-maker influenced by others in the sector?** Many, particularly larger and institutional, grant-makers play an active role in shaping policy and debate concerning issues in their fields of interest. Look for any speaking roles or presences at conferences and forums, or any evidence of co-working with other grant-makers (such as jointly producing reports or co-funding projects) that may be influential on the grant-maker's own activities.

- **Are there any clues about the grant-maker's approach to risk?** Some funders are explicit about their intention to take risks and fund radical work that pushes boundaries or supports emerging needs in innovative ways. Others are more conventional and adopt more traditional approaches to their grant-making. The grant-maker's chosen funding approach can have implications for the way that you describe your project and your organisation, the kind of language that you use, and how you emphasise specific elements of your project's activities.

The how

This part of the research explores the grant-maker's approach processes. Looking at the *how* tells you what you need for each of the succeeding stages in the approach cycle (see figure 1.1).

Key research questions you can use to understand a funder's processes are:

- **What are the application procedures?** Generally, the more formal the funder (for example, larger grant-makers, institutional funders and statutory funders), the more formal and detailed the proposal submission will need to be. Be clear on the process, noting any initial expressions of interest or outline proposals that need to come first – and of course the deadlines for these and any funding calls. There may be published guidelines on what your proposal needs to include, such as maximum page and word counts, or you may need to use a specific application form rather than submitting a freestyle proposal. Funders may also have preferences about how proposals are submitted, such as by email or by post.

- **What are the time frames?** It's not much use if you find a fantastic funder to approach but the grants won't be dispersed until six months after you need the funding (and note that most grant-makers will not fund work retrospectively). Explore how the grant-making cycle works for a particular funder, noting at what point the main decision-makers make their final decision (if known). Also be sure you understand when the funder might expect to receive progress updates down the line to be sure you would be able to deliver these.

- **Are there any clues about how you can approach the grant-maker?** Information about key individuals' networks and connections, as well as any personal interests and their lifestyle, will be central to shaping the way you go about building a relationship. This kind of information is especially helpful when dealing with those funders that state that they don't accept unsolicited applications, as research-based information can help you to find a different way to connect.

- **What kind of acknowledgement would the grant-maker need?** Some funders are quite explicit about this – for example, corporate foundations may wish to have their company's brand visibly associated with yours on websites and social media. In such cases, it is

> We once had to abandon a planned proposal to a major grant-maker that would have been a significant grant for emergency aid materials. The grant-maker desired a level of visibility – specifically its name printed on materials such as blankets and food parcels – that would have undermined our impartiality as an aid organisation.
>
> **Major gifts fundraiser**

appropriate to include within your proposal details of the funder acknowledgement you're offering. Additionally, note any clear acknowledgement requirements for your own use later, when you're thanking the funder and planning your stewarding. Looking at how other grantees have publicly acknowledged support from this funder can also give you some helpful clues. It is important to uncover this information at this early stage, in case you cannot fulfil the funder's acknowledgement requirements.

- **Are there any stewardship clues?** Keep a note of anything your research tells you about what might make the funder feel involved, inspired and nurtured as a partner in your work. Information about personal interests and activities of key individuals (for example, the kinds of events they might attend) can provide handy insights when it comes to planning stewardship after receiving a grant. Thinking about stewardship clues at this early stage will be helpful for planning ahead.

That's a lot of questions, and your research won't always be able to answer all of them, but these are the things you're aiming to uncover. It is important to note the data protection implications of all of these questions – particularly concerning research into individuals – and to comply with the current data protection legislation. This is explored in more detail later on in this chapter (see page 47).

Where to look

You will find a lot of the factual information needed to answer the questions raised in the previous sections on a grant-maker's website, if there is one, or through examining its annual accounts for financial indicators (usually available via the relevant charity regulator's website). Of course, the best source of information is from the horse's mouth, and calling an assigned correspondent or administrator is an obvious way to ask any clarifying questions – particularly about the *how* and proposal submission procedures. But for the softer, more intuitive information about key individuals and the best ways to build good funder relations, there are other tools that can shed some light, especially on the *who* questions. A simple check on a search engine may uncover a lot of soft information about a funder, particularly if any media articles or social media links come up featuring projects, activities or key individuals' recreational interests – these can help you to build a wider picture of someone's motivations and influences. Just be aware that information you find on the internet is not always reliable, so be cautious about which sources you trust. An individual's public presence on a social media website such as Facebook, Instagram, LinkedIn or Twitter can provide useful insights, although do check privacy settings and be cautious about capturing any inappropriate or excessive data as this could put you at odds with data protection legislation (see page 47).

In addition to the research tools we looked at in chapter 2 (some of which will be handy again here), the following resources are widely used by fundraising researchers:

- ***Who's Who* guides** provide biographical data on influential people around the world and are usually available for free from libraries. There are UK (www.ukwhoswho.com) and global versions, such as *Who's Who in America* (see www.marquiswhoswho.com) and *World Who's Who* (www.worldwhoswho.com).

- **Rich lists** such as the Sunday Times Rich List, the Forbes 400 and the Bloomberg Billionaires Index rank ultra-high-net-worth individuals and often detail personal and philanthropic interests.

- **Companies House** (www.gov.uk/government/organisations/companies-house) provides business and directorships information.

- **Debretts** (www.debretts.com) offers helpful information about British society, including peerages and lineages.

- **Livery Companies** of the City of London and their associated charitable funds are listed in a helpful online directory (see www.liverycompanies.info).

- **Online information directories** can be useful for confirming names and addresses of key individuals (see, for example, www.192.com).

Although not an extensive list, these sources should provide you with a great start. Most of them are free to access, whether directly or through your local library. In the case of paid-for subscription services, it is worth asking whether you can try the service for free for a trial period to see how it works for you. There are also helpful guides available to purchase, such as Mathew Iredale's excellent book *Prospect Research: How to find major donors to support your charity*[2] (aimed at major donor fundraising but with lots of relevant advice for research into grant-makers) and Chris Carnie's *Find the Funds: A new approach to fundraising research*,[3] which is an older book but a bit of a classic with useful ideas and techniques.

As in the initial prospecting stage we explored in chapter 2, you may have a specialist in-house team that can support you in funder research. If you have the budget, you could also consider outsourcing detailed research into particularly significant prospects to a consultancy with specific expertise that can fulfil various research requests.

Finally, some of your key research will happen on the job – at the same time as building a relationship with a funder. Some information you could never find on the internet or by other means will come to light through your direct conversations and interactions. These are the real golden nuggets of information, not least because they will be insights that others competing for the same funds may not have, and it is also likely that softer information will be particularly helpful in shaping your approach.

> Once, I got talking to the trustee of a grant-making foundation at a conference, and through our conversation learned that the foundation had determined not to make any new commitments that year, but that the trustees would be explicitly looking at new grantees the following year – this information hadn't been disclosed anywhere else or even by the foundation's administrator.
>
> Grants fundraiser

In this way, research is always ongoing, as you'll be learning new information about your funder all the way through the approach cycle. Throughout the process, you will be handling a lot of detail, and the next section looks at the best way to keep it organised, fresh and current.

A profile template

The most helpful way to manage all the information you continuously gather is to keep an active record on file that is regularly reviewed and updated (with a version date, so you can see how recently the record was updated). Putting everything relevant into a profile document will keep it all in one place and prevent bits of information getting lost among all your other work.

Populating a template like the one illustrated in table 3.1 is a great way of gathering and storing funder research findings. You can expand or condense the template according to the significance of the funder – for example, you might want a lengthy, heavily detailed profile for a major funder, or more of a brief snapshot for a smaller one. You might want to set a level at which prospects automatically get an in-depth research profile compiled (such as prospects with at least £10,000 grant capacity), depending on the size of your organisation and your capacity. Finally, the template can also be adapted to your organisation if extra or different sections would be useful.

Remember that you're not just filling this out for the sake of it, so capture the information that is relevant to the three things we established at the start of this chapter: the approach you'll take with the funder, the shaping of the proposal itself and the way you'll manage the ongoing relationship.

TABLE 3.1 Example funder profile template

Funder's research profile	
Date profile last updated	
Funder's name	
Address, contact details, website	
Trustees or decision-making directors	
Key staff (e.g. names and roles)	
Grant-making information (e.g. other grantees, financials, giving interests/criteria)	
Relevant detail on key individuals, such as staff and decision-makers (e.g. name, date of birth, family, education, employment, directorships, other trusteeships, social and recreational interests, honours, estimated net worth, connections)	
Giving history to our organisation (e.g. current/ lapsed/new prospect, including prior grant details)	
Giving history to other organisations (e.g. brief summary of grant expenditure and typical or noteworthy grants)	
Known links to or experience of our organisation	
Relevant media articles (e.g. links or precis of articles)	
Flagged risk factors (e.g. any potential ethical conflicts or reputational risks)	
Estimated grant capacity (e.g. £10,000)	
Estimated propensity (e.g. high, medium, low)	

Even for major funding prospects, you may not need to include full details in each section, such as exhaustive information on each and every trustee. Use your judgement as to what it is relevant and useful to record. You may also wish to include your qualification rating, if you have one from running the prospect through the qualifying process outlined in chapter 2 (see page 31), as a useful indicator of how much of a hot prospect the funder is for your work. Note that this rating may also have changed a bit after your in-depth research (and remember that qualifying is an intuitive exercise rather than a hard-and-fast rule for prioritising funders).

The section on risk is there to flag up any conflicts of interest that could arise from a potential partnership with a grant-maker. Let's say you've discovered a brilliant new prospect and your research has uncovered a good fit with your charitable objectives as well as some handy connections to a couple of the funder's trustees. You have also discovered, however, that the grant-maker receives the majority of its income from its investments in a tobacco company. If you are a charity working with people affected by cancer, this might pose somewhat of an ethical dilemma and present a reputational risk to your organisation if you accepted a grant from this funder. These kind of risks, even less blatant potential risks (such as negative press associations), need to be flagged up and addressed internally so a decision can be made about whether to proceed with the approach. See chapter 9 (page 150) for a closer look at managing ethical dilemmas and the due diligence required to avoid them, which is becoming increasingly important for fundraising charities.

Setting limits

Researching a funder can be quite fun. You might start off scrolling through a grant-maker's website, check its published accounts and then look through the information on the sources mentioned above to find out more about the individuals involved… and before you know it, one lead has led to another lead and you've clicked your way down a bit of a rabbit hole. Setting a limit – essentially being aware of whether information is actually useful to you or not – is worthwhile to save you wasted time and energy. Finding out that Mr Bloggs plays golf at the same club as your chair of trustees, for example, is very helpful. Finding out that his favourite colour is blue and that he won the egg-and-spoon race at his primary school sports day is probably not.

The other potential hazard is spending so much time researching funders that you never actually get around to approaching them. Hopefully your research will uncover enough useful intelligence to inform the way you go about the subsequent stages of your approach, but you won't always discover a golden key to connect with somebody. And sometimes you'll look everywhere but spend most of the time with your forehead on your desk, because there seems to be very little information available anywhere. Some grant-makers are much harder to research than others and some intentionally remain obscure, either of which will tell you a few things about their style as a funder. So, if you're stuck in a research rut and it's actually preventing you from taking the next step, you may have to call it a day and just move on.

A note on data protection

Great record-keeping of all your gleaned research information is absolutely crucial. For starters, not only will you not want to lose all your hard work, but also you won't want to have to repeat it if you approach the same funder again later down the line. More importantly, though, any use of funder information must abide by the latest data protection rules.

In the UK, the General Data Protection Regulation (GDPR) and the Data Protection Act 2018 make up the legislation covering how personal data – information that relates to an individual (such as a trustee or decision-maker) – is stored and used across all sectors. For fundraisers, the legislation has significant implications for how research findings are treated. It means that the use of any information that relates to individuals who can be identified in any way (not only by their name) has to adhere to the lawful bases and principles of the GDPR.

Lawful bases

Consent and legitimate interest

Recording personal data has to have a valid legal basis. There are six bases stated in the GDPR that you could rely on, but the two that are most relevant for fundraisers are consent and legitimate interest.

Consent means that the individual has given permission for you or your organisation to process their personal data. Their consent has to be freely given, clear, easy for them to withdraw and fully recorded as evidence.

The tricky issue with consent for grant-seekers is that you will be researching funders before you know whether you are going to approach them, and asking for consent would often undermine the whole point of the research. Let's say you ask Mr Bloggs whether he consents to you storing information about him because you've discovered he's connected to one of your trustees and you'd like to develop a relationship so that you can eventually ask for a big grant from his trust... but Mr Bloggs currently has no idea who you are, so this rather puts him off. The request for consent has now undermined the purpose. This is where you can look at legitimate interest instead.

Legitimate interest is often the most appropriate lawful basis for grants fundraisers processing personal data as long as you can justify why you are doing it. If you can show that capturing research data is necessary for what you are trying to achieve, because you need to find funders and understand them to tailor your approach in order to secure funding, then this can be considered legitimate interest. Moreover, funders expect grant-seekers to do their research before initiating an approach, which is also a strong justification under the basis of legitimate interest.[4]

Your data protection policy

These lawful bases must be determined before you begin any data processing and they need to be clearly outlined in your organisation's data protection policy. Within this document, your organisation's stated purposes for data processing should include specifics relating to grants fundraising. This should encompass what information you collect on trustees and other individuals associated with grant-makers, and the ways in which you conduct this research, including all of your data sources and any other prospecting tools you use (such as peer reviews; see page 28).

Your privacy notice

Your organisation is also legally required to have a privacy notice that is in the public domain (such as on your website). This must clearly state your purposes (as above) as well as the details of your legitimate interests if this is your chosen lawful basis. The relevant parts of the privacy notice also need to be provided to the individuals being researched at an appropriate time in your relationship with them. The GDPR sets out time frames for the provision of this information: (a) within one month, (b) when you first communicate or (c) before you share the information with someone else.[5] While some charities provide this fair processing information within a month, many others work to planned time frames for approaching the grant-maker and connecting with the individuals. In taking this approach, they are relying on an associated part of the GDPR, which states that you do not have to provide fair processing information if it will render impossible or seriously impair the achievement of the objectives of the processing. In other words, writing to a potential funder too early could undermine the purpose of the research (as in our example with Mr Bloggs), since grants fundraising typically has a long lead time from research through to approach. It is up to organisations to decide their own policy in relation to the GDPR in this regard; however, whatever you decide, it is important – legally and ethically – to issue a privacy notice to the individual at the earliest appropriate opportunity.

The six principles

Once you have established the legal basis to use, you also need to ensure your processing of personal data abides by the six principles of the GDPR. According to these principles, any personal data must be:

- processed lawfully, fairly and transparently;
- collected for specified, explicit and legitimate purposes;
- limited to what is necessary, adequate and relevant;
- kept accurate and up to date;
- kept for no longer than is necessary;
- processed safely and securely.

In summary, the principles mean that you have to manage personal data carefully, regularly updating it and ensuring you have a clear and justifiable reason to be holding it. The qualification process (see page 31) is helpful here, as you will only carry out detailed research on funders you have identified as good prospects; thus, you will have the justification for why you are holding that level of information. Similarly, you should only record as much information as is absolutely necessary for your fundraising purposes, which fits with the idea of setting research limits (discussed on page 46) and will ensure that you only capture what is useful for your approach planning.

The last principle cannot be overstated. Be sure to password-protect your research profiles and keep hard copies in a locked filing cabinet, so that only those who are authorised can access them. It's also worth putting a note on the top of documents containing funder information (perhaps in red font) along the lines of 'Confidential – for internal use only', to be clear that such documents absolutely must not be shared more widely.

Apart from avoiding obvious embarrassment, it really is a matter of both legal obligation and respect to prevent research data from falling into the wrong hands, so it's worth keeping profiles and event

> Be careful when printing funder information, such as a research profile, to ensure it doesn't loiter on a printer or get left somewhere accidentally. Years ago I had a colleague who went to meet with a grant-maker at the house of one of its trustees and innocently took along the trustee's research profile in her bag. Upon returning to the office, she was mortified to find the document missing from her notes. The trustee found it on their sofa and, luckily, was very gracious about the incident; others may understandably have been less forgiving!
>
> **Major gifts fundraiser**

briefings (which often contain biographies of attendees) securely at the office and shredding them when they are no longer needed.

Special category data

Data protection can sometimes get quite tricky for fundraisers, as we can come into possession of sensitive information through one-to-one conversations. A funder or connector might reveal information about someone's health, for example, or other personal information that is not publicly available. When this is irrelevant to your work or your funding approach, it shouldn't be recorded at all. However, sometimes it *is* relevant, such as if you learn that someone has experience of a particular health condition and your charity works to prevent that particular condition. This, along with any other sensitive information you record about a person (such as their race or ethnic origin, sexuality, political opinions or religious beliefs), is called special category data and needs to be processed particularly carefully. Even an inference – guessing something related to one of the above areas – could be counted as special category data and will usually require the consent of the individual before it can be recorded.

Ensuring compliance

All of the GDPR-related points above apply to any instance where we note down information on any individuals, including in a database, in files and even a scribble in a notebook. A good rule of thumb, for anything you record, is to ask, 'Would I be happy with the person reading this, if they were to request it?' – by law, any individual is within their rights to see personal data you hold on them.

Bear in mind that data protection is also relevant when you collate case study information from beneficiaries. Any stories, quotes and photographs that are used in fundraising materials, such as your proposal, must be used with the full permission of the person (or their estate in the case of a deceased person, although that is ethical practice rather than a legal requirement). If you don't already have one, make sure your organisation has a standard consent form for such permissions that can be signed and kept securely on file.

Data protection is a vast and complex area, and this section provides only a very brief summary of the data protection concerns relating to fundraising from grant-makers. It should not be taken as legal advice and does not cover the many and varied rules covered fully in the legislation that you may need to comply with. There is a lot of helpful guidance on the Information Commissioner's website (www.ico.org.uk) and also a fantastic book by Paul Ticher, *Data Protection for Voluntary Organisations*, which is well worth reading for a more thorough understanding of the GDPR.[6] Additionally, the UK's Fundraising Regulator provides a Code of Practice (www.fundraisingregulator.org.uk), which includes rules you need to adhere to in relation to each fundraising discipline in addition to the GDPR. It is important to make sure that you and your organisation are up to date with both recommended practice and legal requirements, and seek help from a professional data protection adviser if required.

Spotlight: are we being nosey?

Good funder research is all about openness and transparency. But how do funders feel about being researched? Even if we are abiding by all the data protection rules and regulations, is there anything uncomfortable or awkward about us developing research profiles on prospective funders?

A paper by Factary set out to consider these questions, examining the use of the GDPR base of legitimate interest and how this sits alongside the understanding and expectations of the funders that we research.[7] The paper explored the role of prospect research with this in mind and found several themes in previously published literature:

- Funders prefer personalised communications over generic ones[8] and want to receive effective and appropriate communications from charities that are aligned with their areas of interest.[9]
- Many funders enjoy the process of supporting charities, but fundraisers need to take account of funders' interests in order to provide them with relevant opportunities for involvement.[10]
- Funders that develop positive relationships with charities have an enriching and satisfying experience of giving, which in turn makes them more likely to give again.[11]

Conversely, findings also revealed that:

- Funders do not like being asked for an inappropriate amount of money or being asked at the wrong time or place.[12]
- Funders expressly do not want to receive inappropriate or unwanted communications.[13]
- Such behaviours from charities lead to a negative funder experience and are likely to discourage further involvement with an organisation.[14]

Additionally, the report *Good Asking* investigated what the benefits of research information are for funders, charities and the wider public.[15] The report's research showed that 90% of fundraisers believe that funder research enables them to better tailor their work and communications according to the priorities and interests of their funders. The report also found that two-thirds of wealthy donors believed that fundraisers having adopted a 'more professional approach' had been a key factor in the progression of philanthropy in the UK.[16] Furthermore, the findings revealed that in the general population, 60% of people who preferred tailored communications from charities also believed that these charities should be able to use publicly available information in order to tailor their approach, such as from online searches and newspaper articles.

Here is what a UK grant-maker has to say on the matter:

> As charitable funders, we have to give our money away and we want to give it to organisations and projects that are going to make a difference. So it is a partnership from the start, and we both bring something important to the table. With this in mind, fundraisers should feel confident in their role and their need to undertake research into the grant-makers they plan to approach for funding. We don't consider it inappropriate to be asked for more detail about our funding criteria and interests, or to be researched to inform an approach – conversely, doing your homework shows us that you have invested time into understanding our priorities, into engaging with us and into making the most appropriate application.
>
> Caroline Taylor, Chief Executive, Essex Community Foundation

Conclusion

Whether or not you have a dedicated fundraising research function within your organisation, there are plenty of tools available to help you dig deeper into the interests, activities and motivations of grant-makers. Research is a crucial stage of the proposal planning process, as understanding who you are applying to will shape all aspects of your approach. In particular, knowing who the decision-makers are – and finding clues to what, or who, may help to influence them – is absolutely central and can make the difference between a cheque and a rejection letter.

In a nutshell…

- In-depth funder research looks at four main elements to inform the approach: the *who*, the *what*, the *why* and the *how* behind grant-makers and their processes.

- Research resources (such as funder lists and guides) are invaluable – and often free to access – to gaining extra insights, especially into any key connections with a grant-maker. These are best recorded in a profile document that can be updated over time.

• Keep it relevant – if the information you've found is not helpful in shaping your approach (or stewardship), you don't need to know it. Ensure you don't get distracted and lost down a rabbit hole in the name of research.

• Be careful how you record your research findings. Check on your organisation's GDPR compliance and ensure you abide by data protection law when handling funder information.

• Good research isn't being nosey or intrusive – it is an important and welcomed part of the approach process. Most grant-makers *expect* you to have made the effort to understand them and to ensure you are not wasting their time.

Notes

1 See, for example, Elisa Shoenberger, 'Why do people Give? That is the billion-dollar question' [web article], BrainFacts.org, www.brainfacts.org/neuroscience-in-society/law-economics-and-ethics/2018/why-do-people-give-that-is-the-billion-dollar-question-112718, 27 November 2018.

2 Mathew Iredale, *Prospect Research: How to find major donors to support your charity*, n.p., Matthew Iredale, 2019.

3 Chris Carnie, *Find the Funds: A new approach to fundraising research*, London, Directory of Social Change, 2000.

4 Beth Breeze, *Good Asking: The role of research in efficient, effective and enjoyable fundraising* [PDF], Institute of Fundraising, 2017, https://kar.kent.ac.uk/65560/1/Good%20Asking-%20the%20role%20of%20research%20in%20efficient%2C%20effective%20and%20enjoyable%20fundraising.pdf, accessed 7 December 2021.

5 See Paul Ticher, *Data Protection for Voluntary Organisations*, London, Directory of Social Change, 2021 for a more detailed analysis of the rules.

6 Paul Ticher, *Data Protection for Voluntary Organisations*, London, Directory of Social Change, 2021.

7 *Legitimate Interests and Prospect Research* [PDF], Factary, 2017, www.factary.com/docs/Factary_Legitimate_Interests_and_Prospect_Research.pdf, accessed 7 December 2021.

8 Sally Bagwell, Lucy de las Casas, Matt Poortvliet and Rob Abercrombie, *Money for Good UK: Understanding donor motivation and behaviour* [PDF], New Philanthropy Capital, 2013, www.thinknpc.org/resource-hub/money-for-good-uk, accessed 7 December 2021.

9 Sarah Lincoln and Joe Saxton, *Major Donor Giving Research Report: A synthesis of the current research into major donors and philanthropic giving* [PDF], Nfp Synergy, 2012, https://nfpsynergy.net/free-report/major-donor-giving-research-report-updated-synthesis-research-major-donors-and, accessed 7 December 2021.

10 Beth Breeze, *Philanthropic Journeys: New insights into the triggers and barriers for long-term giving and volunteering* [PDF], Centre for Philanthropy, University of Kent, 2014, https://research.kent.ac.uk/philanthropy/wp-content/uploads/sites/2278/2019/06/philanthropic-journeys.pdf, accessed 7 December 2021.

11 Beth Breeze and Theresa Lloyd, *Richer Lives: Why rich people give*, London, Directory of Social Change, 2013; Laura Edwards, *A Bit Rich? What do the wealthy think about giving?* [PDF], Institute for Public Policy Research, 2002, www.ippr.org/files/images/media/files/publication/2011/05/abitrich_1311.pdf, accessed 7 December 2021; Sarah Lincoln and Joe Saxton, *Major Donor Giving Research Report: A synthesis of the current research into major donors and philanthropic giving* [PDF], Nfp Synergy, 2012, https://nfpsynergy.net/free-report/major-donor-giving-research-report-updated-synthesis-research-major-donors-and, accessed 7 December 2021; Sally Bagwell, Lucy de las Casas, Matt Poortvliet and Rob Abercrombie, *Money for Good UK: Understanding donor motivation and behaviour*, New Philanthropy Capital, 2013, www.thinknpc.org/resource-hub/money-for-good-uk, accessed 7 December 2021.

12 Sarah Lincoln and Joe Saxton, *Major Donor Giving Research Report: A synthesis of the current research into major donors and philanthropic giving* [PDF], Nfp Synergy, 2012, https://nfpsynergy.net/free-report/major-donor-giving-research-report-updated-synthesis-research-major-donors-and, accessed 7 December 2021; Adrian Sargeant and Elaine Jay, *Fundraising Management: Analysis, planning and practice*, London, Routledge, 2014; Laura Edwards, *A Bit Rich? What do the wealthy think about giving?* [PDF], Institute for Public Policy Research, 2002, www.ippr.org/files/images/media/files/publication/2011/05/abitrich_1311.pdf, accessed 7 December 2021.

13 Sally Bagwell, Lucy de las Casas, Matt Poortvliet and Rob Abercrombie, *Money for Good UK: Understanding donor motivation and behaviour*, New Philanthropy Capital, 2013, www.thinknpc.org/resource-hub/money-for-good-uk, accessed 7 December 2021.

14 Adrian Sargeant and Elaine Jay, *Fundraising Management: Analysis, planning and practice*, London, Routledge, 2014.

15 Beth Breeze, *Good Asking: The role of research in efficient, effective and enjoyable fundraising* [PDF], Institute of Fundraising, 2017, https://kar.kent.ac.uk/65560/1/Good%20Asking-%20the%20role%20of%20research%20in%20efficient%2C%20effective%20and%20enjoyable%20fundraising.pdf, accessed 7 December 2021.

16 *Ibid.*, p. 13.

CHAPTER FOUR

Planning the approach

Introduction

There's a quote popularly attributed to Abraham Lincoln: 'Give me six hours to chop down a tree and I will spend the first four sharpening the axe.'[1] Abe would have loved the third stage in the approach cycle (see figure 1.1), as it is all about good preparation. Careful planning is the bridge between understanding your prospective funder and engaging with them, as it both makes sure you are ready for the approach and works out exactly how you're going to do it.

> Planning and strategy are key to ensuring that you know whom you are approaching, why and what your desired outcomes will be. It is worth taking the time at the beginning to plan out your approach, to put yourself in the position of the trustee or grants manager, and to consider what will make your application stand out.
>
> Kate Billingham Wilson, Head of Partnerships and Philanthropy, ABF The Soldiers' Charity

This stage is also enormously valuable for those trickier grant-maker approaches – when the funder doesn't accept unsolicited applications. Here is where clever, strategic planning is your ally. Strategic planning will use all of the research you did in the previous stage (see chapter 3), maximising connections and opportunities, and mapping out how to either get in front of an elusive funder or have them find you.

The main questions to ask when planning a specific funder approach are:

- What are we asking the funder for?
- Who needs to be involved in making the approach?
- When is the right time to do it?
- Do we have everything we need before we begin the approach?

This chapter explores the last question first, as this will ensure that all of our ducks are in a row before we proceed.

Following the recipe

The beginning of the previous chapter discussed how research provides the recipe to enable you to plan an approach. This analogy is apt, not least because of our sponge cake model (see figure 1.2) but also because so much of the process is about using the necessary ingredients in quantities and ways that align with your prospective funder's needs. Before you begin approaching a funder, it is important to ensure that there are certain core things in the cupboard.

Recipe for the perfect approach[2]

Dry ingredients

- 250g identified and evidenced need
- 1 tbsp organisational readiness
- 150g freshly prepared budget
- 100ml beneficiaries
- 50g simple outcomes
- 50g realistic impacts

Optional toppings

- 100g peer-to-peer connection
- 15ml innovation
- 25ml creative risk
- 50g activities and/or equipment

Directions

Blend dry ingredients well. Carefully fold in outcomes and impacts. Bake in a pre-heated oven at 200°C. Let cool overnight. Optional: while warm, sprinkle with connection, innovation, creative risk, activities or equipment to ensure a unique treat. Keep secure for up to six months.

Adapted from Deanna Wolf's blog post on MoneyTreeFundraising.co.uk

While this is a bit of fun, this recipe represents the premise for a strong funder approach. The crucial point is that all of these ingredients need to be worked out *in advance* of any proposition, to ensure you are organisationally ready for grants fundraising before moving on to the engagement stage. The following sections explore some of these core ingredients in more detail.

Background information

Funders are likely to have specific questions about your organisation. These may come up in conversation once you have begun engaging and liaising with them, or you may be required to answer them within your funding proposal. Collating a fact-file is a useful way of gathering such fundamental background information, so you have it on hand and are ready to respond to queries. If you don't have one already, put together a document of frequently asked questions and general facts covering the following information about your organisation:

- **history**, including when your organisation was founded, by whom and any key historical events;
- **vision and mission statements;**
- **status**, including charity registration, company and VAT registration numbers, and descriptions of other relevant statuses, registrations and institutional memberships;
- **governance**, including who makes up your board and a short biography of each trustee, plus the members of any management committees;
- **staff and volunteers**, including how many are full time and part time, and number of volunteer hours per year;
- **income and expenditure** – a basic breakdown of your overall numbers;
- **latest annual accounts** and **reserves** information, including your organisation's policy for reserves levels (see page 60);
- **business plan** or **organisational strategy**;
- **fundraising plan**, ideally evidencing a wide support base to show that you are not too heavily reliant on a sole income stream;
- **risk management policy**;
- **unique selling points**, such as being the only organisation that tackles a particular issue or that works in a particular location;
- **common objections** to funding your work and **compelling rebuttals** to those objections, such as being a large organisation that enjoys a lot of public support or working to prevent a disease that is relatively unknown.

Keep this on file and make sure you are well versed in the details. For charities that have been around for a long time, and certainly those with large fundraising departments, it may be easier to gather this internal background information. Smaller organisations, and especially those that are new, may have to work harder to ensure that everything is ready for a funder approach. It is worth the time investment, as many of these topics will come up time and again in funding application forms and it's handy to keep all of the information in one place. It is also worth reviewing your fact-file periodically, annually at the least, to ensure it is up to date.

Most of the 'dry ingredients' in the recipe relate specifically to the project you are looking to raise funds for, and we will return to these in chapter 6, which deals with developing the proposal document. In the meantime, we'll take a closer look at overall organisational readiness, which includes assuring funders of your organisation's necessity, credibility and reputation. Funders want to see that your organisation exists to address an identified need and that there is a strong basis of evidence for that need. Alongside that, you need to demonstrate that externally your organisation is perceived as trustworthy, having its house in order and best placed to carry out its particular work.

Evidence of need

Charities do what they do because they acknowledge and are addressing particular issues: their identified need. It is one thing to know that a problem exists but another to have it substantiated. This is 'evidence of need', and it will likely be one of the first topics a funder will want you to address before they even consider your proposal. If you work for the Hedgehog Rescue Association, for example, you may be very passionate about the welfare of hedgehogs and know that our spiny garden friends need to be protected. But how do you know? Or, more to the point, how does the funder know? It is not enough to assume that just because you know there are hedgehogs in gardens and bonfires on Guy Fawkes Night, that the hedgehogs get stuck in bonfires. You require – and so do your funders – strong evidence to back up this claim.

Evidence of need can be either quantitative or qualitative, and ideally a mix of both. Key facts, figures and statistics are especially helpful – such as '19% of children in England and Wales experience online bullying between the ages of 10 and 15'[3] – and should include the local, regional, national or global picture where relevant. Statistics can back up anecdotal evidence or a description of the issue, although both of these should be based on expert knowledge and experience. Sources of this evidence could be research, consultation, feedback from surveys or questionnaires involving beneficiaries or others with direct experience of the need.

However it is collated, your evidence must be robust and reliable, revealing the nature of the issue and why it is a problem for your particular beneficiary group, as well as the scale and how widespread it is. It is also helpful to capture any social trends that affect the issue, for example 'the current pressure on hospital beds means that by the year 2030 the NHS will be unable to cope with the needs of the ageing population'[4]. This will set your evidence of need in context. Do also reference the sources of your cited evidence, to provide additional reliability and impact.

Showing your credibility

Before you approach anybody, you need to be sure they will believe in your organisation's ability to run itself well, as much as the particular project for which you are seeking support. Having credibility means that funders can trust that yours is the right organisation to deliver the work and to manage their funds responsibly. This includes good governance, professionalism and having effective systems in place to track grants.

One of the best ways to demonstrate credibility is to be able to communicate your organisation's track record. This involves collating statistics, trends, evaluation reports, case studies, and any positive press or media coverage that proclaims your successes and achievements. Quotations and positive feedback from beneficiaries and any main financial sponsors who endorse your work (such as other funders) are also brilliant sources that can attest to your organisation's integrity. You could also add these to your fact-file and be ready to use them in conversations with funders as well as at the proposal stage.

What if yours is a new organisation with little or no track record? There are other ways to demonstrate credibility without having a long-standing history to your name, if you get a little creative. One of the best ways is to lean on the expertise of those involved with your work – senior staff, project managers, trustees and advisers. People of note or those who are highly regarded in their field are a great asset to your organisation, and their quotes or letters of support can raise your credibility by association. Similarly, if you can show a high calibre of committed staff, volunteers (appropriately trained and supported), board members or patrons, the implication is that your organisation is well run and managed efficiently. List any prominent people who are linked to your work (with their permission) on your website and letterheads and in any publications. If you are able to show that your programmes are based on a successful model, even if it has been developed elsewhere, this can also be a powerful tool, particularly if you can explain how you have adapted the model for the specific issues you are tackling. Any early press coverage about what you are doing is additionally very helpful. You can use all of these angles to give a funder confidence in your organisation's ability to deliver.

Whether new or established, all organisations need to be able to show high-quality business planning, including long-term programme and funding plans, and to demonstrate that they are financially sound. Any prospective funder will want to see that your accounts are in order – filed on time to the relevant regulator – and ideally reflecting that your organisation is financially healthy, secure, solvent and making good use of its funds.

One of the questions that is often asked of charities is around their level of reserves. A reasonable level of reserves is generally considered to be the equivalent of between three and twelve months' worth of running costs. Any less than three months may be considered risky, as funders will want to see that a sensible precaution has been taken should your organisation get into difficulty. More than a year's worth, however, may need to be explained as it could look like you are sitting on a lot of cash and don't really need additional funding.[5] There can be perfectly good reasons for higher reserves, such as holding restricted funds for a specific purpose (for a capital project, for example); if this is the case for your organisation, make sure you have a very clear explanation prepared. As indicated in the fact-file contents list (see page 57), many funders will routinely ask to see a reserves policy statement. This can be a simple statement of no more than two sides of A4, addressing four basic questions:

- **Why do you need reserves?** For example, to safeguard against financial problems or to invest in the organisation's development.

- **What level of reserves is appropriate for your organisation?** For instance, three months' worth of running costs? Six months? More?

- **How will you build up a reserve within this policy, if required?** For example, the trustees may decide to allocate an amount of annual surplus for the next few years.

- **How will progress be monitored?** For instance, through the scrutiny of a finance sub-committee.

Talk to your finance department or financial adviser to check that these points are all covered in your policy and that the policy can be shared with funders if requested.

Growing your reputation

One of the great things about the grant-making community is that its members talk to each other. Many grant-makers will be well aware of who funds whom, and which organisations have a particularly good (or less good) reputation in their area of work. It is very helpful, therefore, if you can get your name known and established as the go-to organisation in your field.

Building a strong reputation does not necessarily mean being a large charity, with your work broadcast on television and promoted on billboards. In fact, this can even be disadvantageous for such charities, as the resulting perception can be that they already have plenty of cash to splash. No matter the size of your organisation and marketing budget, the aim is to become front of mind for funders interested in your area and recognised as an organisation that makes a real, sustainable difference to the issue at hand.

Getting your name out there has a further advantage. At the end of chapter 2, we saw that one of the main routes to funding from grant-makers is when they make the initial contact (see page 33). Such funders are proactive in seeking out potential grantees doing work that piques their interests, so being visible and easy to find should be an important part of your strategy. This is also the case for those seemingly elusive funders which specify that they will not accept any unsolicited applications. If the hunt for a connection is coming up short, you will want to be sure that these kinds of funder are going to come across your work if there is any chance of you forming a relationship.

One of the best ways of being visible is to get on the circuit. This means attending, participating in, and speaking at conferences and events where prospective grant-makers are likely to be. Identify senior and programme staff who are particularly good at talking about your work (or the problem it addresses), have a solid reputation themselves and can speak with conviction. More generally, having your organisation's voice heard in the media – such as in articles, on television and on social media (including at a local or regional level) – increases the likelihood of a funder coming across your work and helps to position your organisation as the expert on a particular topic. A useful tactic is to set up these opportunities yourself, by actively hosting events such as open days or round-table discussions, where invitees can come along to hear and participate in expert conversations about relevant themes. An unsolicited event invitation is not the same as an unsolicited funding proposition, so this can be a great reason to make contact while also giving your organisation a platform as a mover and shaker in your area.

Even large and well-publicised charities need to do this, especially if they are looking for funds from grant-makers for programmes of work that may not be that obviously connected with their organisation:

> Most people have heard of our organisation. The work we do, however, is very broad ranging and we are often fundraising for projects that people might not immediately associate with our name. We needed funding for a palliative care project, for example, working with children living with HIV/AIDS in sub-Saharan Africa, but most

> funders with a specific interest in palliative care would be unlikely to think of us as an obvious grantee. So we decided to put on a round-table event at our office, co-hosted with a trust that specialised in palliative care, and invited other funders and people with a particular interest in the topic to hear about the project and discuss the issue together. It showed those attending that we had expertise in that area, opened up conversations with new potential funders and promoted the excellent work of the project all in one go.
>
> Luke Brocket, Head of Private Foundations, UNICEF UK

It is worth noting that putting on such events, where the focus is on growing your reputation in the field, might appear to be a distraction from front-line fundraising. You may need to convince some senior or programme staff that this kind of activity is an important part of a grants fundraising strategy.

Your organisation's website should also be very clear about what you do, look professional and include engaging case studies as part of reputation-building, particularly as this is one of the first places a new funder is likely to go to learn about you. Similarly, being able to publicly demonstrate a good record for working well with other organisations, such as celebrating partnerships on social media, is also part of showing your wares and getting noticed.

What, who and when?

We have looked at the background preparation that is necessary for grants fundraising readiness. The next planning questions look at the details of the approach, or the ask itself.

How much is too much?

Your funder research findings (see chapter 3) should inform what exactly you are asking for funds towards, depending on the kind of funding the grant-maker prefers to provide and how that matches the needs of your work. It could be for a specific item of a project's budget, a contribution towards the project as a whole or indeed funds to cover the entire project budget. The financial information from this research will also frame the amount you are looking for from a particular funder. You will need to consider the grant-maker's giving capacity and the types of grant usually dispersed, such as one-off grants or those given over multiple years. The option of asking for funding over a number of years can be a good way of requesting a larger grant where the full amount may be too much of a stretch for a funder's grant-making capacity in one go. It is also a useful back-up plan; sometimes a funder may be interested in supporting a project but is too committed to other grantees at the time to support yours at the desired level. Therefore, suggesting a grant is dispersed over a few years can be a great way of spreading the cost for the funder while still bringing them on board as a partner for your work.

It is usually better to over-ask than to under-ask. So, if it is not clear how much would be the most appropriate amount to request, err on the optimistic side. If you are hoping for a £50,000 grant, for example, but are concerned that this would be right at the top end of a funder's giving capacity, it is better to ask for the £50,000 that you really need than to ask for less for fear of putting the funder off. A grant-maker may give you less than you ask for, but you definitely won't receive £50,000 if you only ask for £10,000. Certainly at this stage, plan for the maximum grant – you can reassess later if it becomes apparent that you are overshooting.

Different strokes for different folks

On page 26 we looked at the different categories of prospective funders, according to their history of giving to your organisation. Extremely lapsed funders – those that have given to you in the past, but very many years ago – will need to be treated as if they were new, cold prospects. As both of your organisations are likely to have changed a lot in that time, your plan will need to involve identifying the current decision-makers and influential individuals, and looking for ways to engage them with the key people in your own charity.

More recently lapsed funders will need a different type of approach, as the focus will be on re-engagement. There will hopefully still be some common ground and connection between your two organisations, but your planning will need to focus on unearthing why the partnership did not continue and how best to reignite it. The introduction of new staff, new projects or new funder priorities can be an excellent reason to be getting back in touch and to rekindle the relationship.

For recent funders that have given in the past year, the focus of your approach planning will be to continue, nurture and grow the funding partnership. Your plan will need to include demonstrating and celebrating the success of the previous grant, as well as exploring any potential for uplifted funding – that is, increasing the funding commitment where possible.

Having these different funder categories in mind is helpful for clarifying the focus of your approach and working out the most effective course of action.

Percussionist and lead violinist

Once you know what you are requesting and how best to go about it, you also need to make a plan about *who* is going to make the approach. As a fundraiser, you are the conductor of the orchestra, but you are not necessarily the lead performer on stage. This means that you may be making all the arrangements, but someone else may be the better front-person.

In the ideal scenario, you will have two or three other roles involved in a grant-maker approach. If you, the fundraiser, are the conductor, then there is also the role of the main performer (let's call them the lead violinist) and the back-up (let's call them the percussionist). This is an adaptation of a concept developed by Fundraising Training Ltd, called 'The Hit Squad' and it might look something like the following.[6]

The percussionist is the one who starts the approach, as they make the introduction between you and the funder. Think of a tap-tap-tap of a cymbal or drum announcing that the music is starting. This person is someone connected but likely external to your organisation, who is known and respected by the funder (or the key individual at the funder, such as a grants director or a core trustee). Perhaps it is one of your current funders, a high-level volunteer or a contact of one of your senior staff. You may have identified the right person for this role through your peer review (described in chapter 2; see page 28) or they may have come to light during your funder research. Their role is simply to make the connection. Be it through a call, letter or face-to-face meeting, they introduce the funder to you and allow you to get that first crucial contact. This is why it is important that they are known and respected by the funder; the funder is taking their word that you are worth an investment of time, or at the very least is willing to do their contact a favour by talking to you.

The lead violinist is the star of the show. This person is someone with strong knowledge of your organisation and the project you are fundraising for. They will also have a solid reputation and, ideally, a level of charisma sufficient to convey your needs with passion and conviction. They may be the project manager, a senior director or even your CEO. They need to be someone who will speak confidently and be comfortable in front of a funder, as they are going to be doing most of the talking in meetings. Unlike the percussionist (the initial connector), their role is to be persuasive. They have the technical answers and a deep understanding of the needs of your beneficiaries, and will be able to reassure the funder about your organisation's management and efficiency.

David Bull CBE has spent over 30 years leading major international non-profit organisations, including UNICEF UK and Amnesty International UK. During this time, David has frequently played this key role in supporting relationships with funders:

> Fundraising is an essential part of any non-profit organisation and I have always considered leadership roles as integral to that process. Many funders, understandably, want to meet the captain of the ship. As a philanthropist once told me, funders support people as much as causes – if they trust and relate to the person who leads the

> organisation, that is a critical element in their decision-making. As a CEO, therefore, it is important to make the time to meet and engage with funders; it isn't optional, and it can't be left entirely to your fundraisers. You need to spend the time to support their efforts and to ensure that you are properly briefed before you go into a meeting with a funder – they will expect you to know your stuff.
>
> David Bull CBE

The other handy thing about having your lead violinist involved is that they will be able to hand over the relationship to you afterwards. Some funders would really prefer to talk directly to the lead violinist most of the time. However, if your lead violinist can make an explicit handover, this will give you permission in the eyes of the funder to be the one who takes the relationship forward.

Working out who the best people for the task are, and how to arrange this sequence of events, is all part of your approach planning. This 'A-Team' kind of collaboration is much more effective than making a cold approach on your own. Your role as the conductor is to identify these other players, fully brief them and then support them as the approach unfolds. Much as in an orchestra, though, yours is not a hidden role. The fundraiser is very much present – listening, observing, taking notes and assuming responsibility for any follow-up actions from face-to-face encounters. It's also not a passive part; it is supplementary but active, co-ordinating everything and taking on the leg work of fulfilling the relationship after the initial conversation. This includes keeping a record of what is discussed and deciding what happens next, even if the next steps are carried out in the lead violinist's or percussionist's name.

Of course, sometimes fundraisers have no choice but to play all of these roles themselves. This is particularly likely to be the case in very small organisations, where you may indeed be the project manager, the fundraiser *and* the CEO! While the ideal scenario will involve different players, it is entirely possible to do it all yourself as a solo performer. However, generally speaking, involving other key people is a more effective and strategic approach – and less likely to leave you playing second fiddle to your competitors.

The roles of both the percussionist and the lead violinist will come back into the picture at later stages (see chapters 7 and 8), specifically when it comes to submitting the proposal and thanking after a grant.

Timings

The last big planning question is 'when' – when is the right time to make your move? Grant-makers often have very clear and specific proposal deadlines (commonly just ahead of trustee meeting dates), which is handy for working backwards as most approaches take somewhere between 6 and 18 months from initial identification to putting in the financial ask. If a project is dependent on grants funding to start, you will need to factor in enough lead time to ensure you can both make the approach *and* learn the outcome before the work is due to begin. For larger and more complicated approaches, it may actually take years of careful planning, engaging and relationship-building before a proposal goes in; for very significant partnerships and sums of money, this can be entirely appropriate.

At other times, you may receive an email alert about a new funding opportunity that is closing very soon – say, in two weeks' time. In this case, a decision has to be made about whether to go in all guns blazing and make the deadline, or wait this round out until a good relationship can be established first. The latter is usually the preferred option, simply because it is likely to result in a larger and longer-term funding partnership, but there are always exceptions. The trick is to weigh up the odds of success while being optimistic and seizing good opportunities when they arise.

Planning your approach timings is also relevant when you are reapplying to a grant-maker if you were previously unsuccessful or are looking to re-approach a lapsed funder. Some grant-makers will ask you to wait a certain period before reapplying after either a previous grant or an unsuccessful application. This is usually due to the numbers of funding requests they receive rather than a desire to put you off. The time delay can be an advantage if used wisely. You can actively search for an extra connection, whether a peer-to-peer link or another engagement opportunity, which could bring the funder closer to your cause.

With this in mind, even if there is no specified time frame for which to wait before reapplying, it is usually a good idea to give it at least six months – probably longer, such as a year – after a previously unsuccessful application. This is to give you time to re-evaluate your approach, re-build the relationship where necessary and amend your proposal plans. Unless you have reason to believe otherwise, assume that the funder's decision would be unlikely to change without you having amended your approach, your proposal or both.

As well as being aware of deadlines, trustee meeting dates and specified time frames, it is also worth considering the funder's own financial year, which will be stated in its published accounts. Some grant-makers will have funds left to disperse towards the end of their financial year, making this a ripe time to be applying. Alternatively, some funding opportunities may be more likely to be successful at the beginning of the funder's new financial year, when a fresh budget is available. It is helpful to be aware of these timings, both during your research and in your subsequent relationship-building, as they can inform your submission planning and help to maximise your opportunities.

Drawing up your approach plan

An approach plan (or 'solicitation plan') is the road map of how you intend to engage, proposition and eventually – if successful – thank and steward your funder. It plots the route for everything else to come in the approach cycle. Creating a plan like this shouldn't be an onerous exercise – much like in the cases of qualifying your prospects (see page 31) and producing in-depth research profiles (see page 44), it should be a live document that you regularly refer to and that genuinely aids your approach.

An approach plan will also be really helpful for future fundraisers so that information and strategy are not lost and then replicated down the line if there is a turnover of staff. It will also help to maintain consistency for the funder, by providing continuity in your charity's communication and engagement activities. An approach plan can be merged with a research profile to make a single longer document if it seems logical – particularly if you would otherwise be duplicating a lot of information across the two. There is no particular right or wrong way to do it, as long as it serves its purpose. Do remember to make sure you're adhering to the data protection legislation we looked at in chapter 3 (see page 47) if you include any personal information within the document.

Table 4.1 shows an example of what a short and simple approach plan might look like for a fictional grant-maker. For larger or more complex approaches, the action steps will be more detailed and numerous, but the principles will remain the same. For plans with many activities across a long period of time, you may also find it helpful to create a timeline of events, such as in the example here. This can help you to visually get a sense of the key points of contact across a year, for instance, and map them against other organisational activities and events. However it is presented, the aim is to plot and capture your plan of action in a format that is easy to read.

TABLE 4.1 Example approach plan

Funder approach plan	
Funder name:	The Big Grants Foundation
Giving history to our organisation:	None – new prospect
Key funder contacts:	Remi G. (Chair of Trustees) Emily H. (Grants Director) Adam K. (Secretary)

Key points from research:	The Big Grants Foundation gives around £400,000 per annum for causes 'alleviating poverty, improving health and empowering young people' nationally. Emily H. oversees all major grants activity. Grants range from £5,000 to £50,000, usually multi-year. Remi G. has been chair for eight years and is known to Simon R., as they attended the same college.
Key relationship holders in our organisation:	Juan S. (Fundraising Manager – keyworker) Kate B. (CEO) Simon R. (Trustee – peer connection)
Proposed ask:	£50,000 over three years, for Building Futures programme.
Action steps:	1. Juan S. to discuss approach with Simon R. at July board meeting and ask to use connection. 2. Juan S. to draft introductory letter from Simon R. to Remi G., including description of Building Futures programmes and upcoming Autumn Gala event – Simon R. to approve and sign. 3. Juan S. to introduce Remi G. and Kate B. at Autumn Gala event – aim for follow-up meeting. 4. Arrange meeting for Kate B. and Juan S. with Remi G. and/or Emily H. – introduction to charity and project and follow up with project visit invitation. 5. Building Futures project visit – Juan S. and either Kate B. or Simon R. to attend. 6. Kate B. to invite Emily H. to January round-table discussion event and also invite Remi G. to Christmas Carols event – seat next to Simon R. 7. Juan S. to submit proposal for March deadline – Kate B. to sign off, Simon R. to sign cover letter and follow up. 8. Kate B. to follow up with Emily H. and invite her to funders' lunch if successful.

Timeline:

Jul	**Aug**	**Sep**	**Oct**	**Nov**	**Dec**	**Jan**	**Feb**	**Mar**	**Apr**	**May**	**Jun**
Draft letter for SR		Autumn Gala event		Project visit	Christmas Carols			Proposal submission	Follow-up		Funders' lunch

Proposed thanks and recognition:	Personal thank-you notes from Kate B. to Emily H. and from Simon R. to Remi G. Named plaque on youth centre building. Invite Emily H. and Remi G. to unveil. Social media acknowledgement with photo of plaque. Invite to funders' lunch in June.

This is your proposed course of action, should everything go as planned, but it is certainly not set in stone. It is highly likely to change over time, as what happens at each point will affect what you do subsequently. The plan is therefore very much a live document. The plan serves to formulate a strategic intention, based on your research findings, to outline the best route to building a good relationship and securing funding success. It also provides a sounding board to keep you on track, and keep key individuals involved and accountable for agreed actions. Finally, simply by writing everything down, it is much more likely that you will actually do the things proposed.[7]

For significant funder propositions, it is helpful to run the plan past any key internal people – perhaps your connector (the percussionist) or programme expert (the lead violinist), if relevant – they may be able to add value or challenge and sense-check any assumptions.

Spotlight: looking for links

Charities may feel that they do not have many, or perhaps any, connections who could help with introductions to grant-makers. However, it only takes one or two people close to your organisation to help with unlocking doors to more-difficult-to-reach funders. In fact, in research conducted by KEDA Consulting, almost a third of charities surveyed said that they had benefitted from a personal introduction to start a funder relationship. Nearly another quarter said that they knew influencers who could endorse their applications but had not benefitted from these relationships yet.[8]

Philanthropy research has clearly established that uncovering these connections is an important part of a successful grants fundraising strategy. In 2002, the Institute for Public Policy Research published one of the first studies on the motivations behind major giving to charities: *A Bit Rich? What do the wealthy think about giving?*[9] The study found that who approached a funder was particularly important, with many funders frequently becoming involved with causes through a friend or acquaintance. Research by Beth Breeze and Theresa Lloyd, outlined in their book *Richer Lives: Why rich people give*, further found that people actually *prefer* to be introduced to a non-profit by a peer, and almost all of the funders interviewed said that they would at least review and respond to a request from someone they knew and respected.[10]

The Open University and St John Ambulance both adopt this strategy in their grants fundraising:

> We find that mapping relationships and networks is absolutely key to unlocking and strengthening funder relationships. This is true despite the fact that many grant-makers make their application processes and interests known at the outset. Advice on what they

look for, the differences between successful and unsuccessful applications, and alignment with their strategic priorities are often best understood through conversations, whether with someone senior in the management team or on the board. We always try to uncover who we know and through whom, to help facilitate such dialogue. In some cases, these key links can also help to champion or sponsor applications where organisations allow for such an approach to be taken.

Jhumar Johnson, Chief of Staff to the Vice-Chancellor, The Open University

For us it's about connecting grant-makers with the work that we do and making it relevant to them as people, as well as to the change their organisation is trying to achieve. It is well known that people give to people, and with St John volunteers in communities across England, we always look to see if we can identify connections and opportunities for a peer-led approach with a funder.

Victoria Ives, Trusts and Statutory Manager, St John Ambulance

Charities also do not need to be large or well known to find people who can help by making introductions, and often these individuals simply need to be asked. Early childhood development charity Best Beginnings has found the peer-to-peer approach to be a very effective way of reaching funders that would otherwise be tricky to engage:

Although we are not a large charity, we have experienced numerous occasions when a door has been opened for us to engage with a funder that we could not have opened on our own. One example of this is when someone at a current funder introduced us to one of their grant-making peers, a trust that does not accept unsolicited applications. After meeting with the trust's representatives, we were invited to apply, which resulted in a grant of £100,000. This was only made possible through the initial peer-to-peer introduction, which came about because of the strong relationship we'd built with our other funder, whose team had developed a deep understanding of our work and were willing to advocate on our behalf.

We are certainly not part of a 'special club' where we have lots of easily accessible connections to grant-makers. We simply ask our own trustees, patrons and supporters about funders they could introduce us to, even if just to allow for exploratory conversations with new prospects, and this reaps huge rewards. In our experience, grant-makers share notes and talk to each other about their experience of the charities they support, so there is extra value to a funder relationship if the funder is willing to support us with peer-led introductions on top of financial support. The trick is to ask.

Alison Baum, CEO and Founder, Best Beginnings

Conclusion

Planning your funder approach can take time, but it is worth the effort to formulate the strongest course of action possible to engage effectively with a grant-maker. This stage is fluid, as your plan is active and may be amended as it unfolds. However, taking a strategic approach can mean the difference between a 'yes' and a 'no', particularly for more elusive funders.

In a nutshell...

- Preparation is key. While it may be tempting to skip from finding a funder to writing a proposal, crafting a strategic approach plan is more likely to result in funding success.

- Ensure you have all your basic ingredients ready. A fact-file is a helpful way of keeping key statistics and answers to frequently asked questions on hand, including evidence of your beneficiaries' needs and your organisation's credibility and reputation.

- Consider who else can play a key role in the funder approach; you are the conductor, but the approach can be strongest when other people take centre stage in the process.

- Your approach plan is your road map. It will plot out how you will carry out each of the subsequent stages from engagement through to stewardship. It will also keep you accountable along the way.

- Unlocking peer-to-peer connections is a powerful approach tool and can make all the difference with engaging harder-to-reach funders.

Notes

1 Although these words have been attributed to Abraham Lincoln over the years, the origin of the quote is unconfirmed. Various versions of the saying have also been credited to an anonymous woodchopper; see 'To cut down a tree in five minutes spend three minutes sharpening your axe' [web article], Quote Investigator, https://quoteinvestigator.com/2014/03/29/sharp-axe, 29 March 2014.

2 Adapted and included with permission from Deanna Wolf, 'A recipe for the "perfect" grant application' [blog post], Money Tree Fundraising, https://moneytreefundraising.co.uk/a-recipe-for-the-perfect-grant-application, 18 September 2018.

3 This is actually true; see 'Online bullying in England and Wales: year ending March 2020' [web page], Office for National Statistics, 2020, www.ons.gov.uk/peoplepopulationandcommunity/crimeandjustice/bulletins/onlinebullyinginenglandandwales/yearendingmarch2020, accessed 27 January 2022.

4 This another true example; see 'Hospital bed numbers – can the downward trend continue?' [web page], The King's Fund, 2017, www.kingsfund.org.uk/blog/2017/09/hospital-bed-numbers, accessed 27 January 2022.

5 See also the Charity Commission for England and Wales's guidance *Charity reserves: building resilience (CC19)* available at www.gov.uk/government/publications/charities-and-reserves-cc19.

6 The original concept was developed as part of a training course by Fundraising Training Ltd; see www.fundraisingtraining.co.uk.

7 See, for example, Mark Murphy, 'Neuroscience explains why you need to write down your goals if you actually want to achieve them' [web article], Forbes, www.forbes.com/sites/markmurphy/2018/04/15/neuroscience-explains-why-you-need-to-write-down-your-goals-if-you-actually-want-to-achieve-them/?sh=57243f387905, 15 April 2018.

8 *Funding Social Change: How can grant-seekers and grant-makers collaborate to better serve our communities?* [PDF], KEDA Consulting, 2021, www.kedaconsulting.co.uk/wp-content/uploads/2021/06/keda_consulting_funding_social_change_a4_50pp_V2.pdf, pp. 17–18, accessed 7 December 2021.

9 Laura Edwards, *A Bit Rich? What do the wealthy think about giving?* [PDF], Institute for Public Policy Research, 2002, www.ippr.org/files/images/media/files/publication/2011/05/abitrich_1311.pdf, accessed 7 December 2021.

10 Beth Breeze and Theresa Lloyd, *Richer Lives: Why rich people give*, London, Directory of Social Change, 2013.

CHAPTER FIVE

Building the relationship

Introduction

In years gone by, the main criterion of a grants fundraiser's job description would have been something like 'excellent writing skills' followed by 'ability to work to deadlines' and 'experience with targets and budgets'. These are important, even critical, aspects of the role. However, increasingly we are seeing more relational elements of the job coming to the fore; 'strong relationship-building skills' and 'confident in face-to-face engagement' are now vying for the top positions on recruiters' wish lists.

This is an excellent shift, as fundraising from grant-makers has often carried the perception of being a desk-based, paper-focused activity, with the emphasis on churning out applications rather than being out and about building relationships. Most charities have recognised that the former is an outdated way of doing things, for the simple reason that behind all grant-makers – of all shapes and sizes, from small family foundations to formal institutional funders – there are people. Therefore, interpersonal relationships are at the very core of what we do.

Successfully building and nurturing funder relationships prior to submitting a proposal is arguably as essential to the entire funding process as the physical written document itself. As mentioned in earlier chapters, relationship-building can uplift lower-level funders to maximise their giving potential to your cause, and it can reignite grant-making from previous, lapsed funders. Finally, it is without doubt the most effective way to secure a grant from a completely new, prospective funder to your organisation.

The bottom layer of the sponge

Chapter 1 talked about the holistic approach to grants fundraising being akin to a sponge cake (see figure 1.2) – two thick layers either side of a jam centre. While the jam is your proposal, the entire bottom sponge layer ('Funder cultivation') is dedicated to getting to know your funder first. This includes detailed research and planning, as we have explored, which both pave the way for the relationship-building – or engagement – phase of the process. Engagement can make all the difference to whether or not your proposal is successful, and particularly whether a long-term, multi-year and mutually enriching funder–charity partnership is established.

> From experience we know that we are more successful when we work building relationships with funders and developing partnerships to achieve a shared goal. It's not about firing off an application – it's about understanding the difference someone wants to achieve and really listening to what they say.
>
> Victoria Ives, Trusts and Statutory Manager, St John Ambulance

Close and mutually beneficial funder–grantee relationships can potentially even lead to the co-creation of the proposal. In such cases, the details of the proposition are worked up together with the funder, even shaping elements of the programmatic activity (although caution is needed in this situation so as not to become funder-led: see page 150 for more on that particular issue).

One of the challenges of this stage is time. It can be tempting to rush through funder engagement, particularly if the project you are seeking funds for is about to begin or is in desperate need of cash to continue. Another tricky situation is where you have identified a good prospect but the deadline is fast approaching and there isn't enough time to do any engagement work before you need to submit something. In this scenario there is a judgement call to make (as discussed on page 66), but it is always worth considering whether it is possible to wait for another funding round: such is the weight of the relationship in the approach.

At this point it is worth mentioning that some charities have a grants fundraising system whereby applications are sent out in bulk. The focus for these organisations is on quantity: getting out as many approaches as possible and using a ratio (for example, 1 in 10 proposals might result in a grant – so if we send out 50 proposals, we might get 5 grants) as a method of projecting potential grants income. This will inevitably work some of the time. However, a focus on quality – making fewer but better, relationship-based approaches – is a much stronger and longer-term strategy. It is also part of the reputation-building we looked at in chapter 4 (see page 60), as grant-makers do absolutely talk to each other: you want to be known for your excellent partnership management and focused approach, rather than as a charity that's always sending in appeals as part of a general fundraising drive.

It's useful to remember the purpose of relationship-building:

- It helps you to better understand a funder's real interests and motivations (and this understanding in turn dictates what you ask for and how you present it in a proposal).
- It refines your approach plan: as you get to know the funder, you gain clarity about what is the best timing for each step and who is the best-placed person to be doing it.

• It puts you front of mind when the proposal eventually lands on the funder's desk, increasing the chance of it being thoroughly considered and reducing the chance of it ending up in the 'maybe' or 'small grants' pile – or, worse, the bin.

Now you know why this stage is so important, let's take a look at how you can increase funder engagement and build strong relationships in practice.

Ways of engaging funders

All grant-makers are different, so the best way of engaging with them will vary from one to another. Your research will hopefully have provided some invaluable clues as what would be appropriate for a given funder, including who the key people are at the grant-maker's end that you want to engage, and who needs to be involved in the process from your end.

For larger grant-makers in particular, where there are multiple staff teams and various influencers and decision-makers, it is likely that your engagement strategy will need to have more than one level. Any gatekeepers – individuals whose role involves control or influence over what gets through to key decision-makers – are likely to be important relationships for you to establish. Effectively building rapport with a gatekeeper can help you to secure meetings with key individuals and ensure that your proposal is seen by the right person at the right time. A top tip here is to be mindful that gatekeepers (such as grants administrators and personal assistants) are adept at dealing with fundraisers and will be absolutely aware of your intention to connect directly with their trustees. The aim is not to get around gatekeepers but to get to know them and help them to learn about you. After all, you have something of value to the cause their organisation exists to support. There is also a difference between being genuine and trying to nobble someone. The latter is usually quite obvious, and something most gatekeepers are likely to resist.

Other useful key relationships are likely to be between the senior staff at your and the grant-maker's organisations. For example, it could be important for your organisation's CEO to get to know the grant-maker's CEO or chair of trustees. Similarly, programme experts (particularly at institutional funders) should get to know their counterparts at your organisation, and have in-depth discussions in their areas of specialism to build credibility and respect between the parties. Having several relational touchpoints across your respective organisations also ensures continuity, so if there is any changeover of staff on either side, there are other warm relationships that remain.

The more personal the engagement, the stronger it will be. Therefore, the more face-to-face interaction a relationship is based on, usually the better. Meetings, events and project visits all provide opportunities for face-to-face engagement, and talking to someone in person will almost always tell you more about them than a conversation over the phone or via email. Likewise, for funders, meeting you and any key staff at your organisation – and especially seeing your work in person – will create knowledge and understanding that will be transformational when it comes to them finally reading your proposal.

> We take every opportunity to speak to and meet with the people behind trusts. This is key to building relationships and positions us to respond to any development within the trust. For example, we had a trust that had given us £5,000 a few times but we knew there was the potential for more. We met with one of the trustees, who was about to become deputy chair. She was encouraging the trustees to give more, larger grants and we went on to apply and receive a grant of £85,000 – 17 times our previous largest grant.
>
> Andy Watts, former Head of Trusts, Sue Ryder

Many grant-makers are very open to meeting with charities and fundraising organisations, but you will need to clearly explain why there is overlap between their interests and yours, and outline the potential for a fruitful partnership. Even those that initially appear more closed to this level of interaction will be much more likely to agree to a meeting if it has been proposed by someone else – this is where the percussionist role we looked at on page 63 and the links you may have identified through your peer review (see page 28) are particularly important. The power of such connections cannot be understated. Asking someone prominent whom you know to make the initial contact, even if they are not personally known by the grant-maker, may still get you space in the busiest of funders' diaries. Much like when it comes to making decisions about the funding itself, a lot of the time grant-makers don't do meetings simply because they haven't been asked.

As an alternative to meeting in person, video calls are an excellent way of gaining face-to-face engagement with a funder, particularly if geographical distance would otherwise make such an encounter difficult. Amid the COVID-19 pandemic, video calls became the essential way of holding a meeting, and this has remained a cost-effective (saving on travel time and expense) and much more normalised way of communicating. The other advantage of video calls is that there can be a helpful disarming effect due to the neutrality of the virtual meeting space – in neither party's office or territory. This is especially the case when someone is working from home, as there is something immediately connecting about being allowed into a personal home space, even if only virtually.

While face-to-face engagement is ideal, strong relationships can also be built successfully over the telephone. It is remarkable how underused this tool can be, especially when so many funders have their contact number listed on the charity regulator's website or, sometimes even more clearly, on their own website. In fact, a survey of UK fundraisers showed that only 16% routinely pick up the phone to speak to a funder when there is a number available; the vast majority (76%) only do so if they have a specific query (and 8% never call funders at all).[1]

Many fundraisers can find phone calls with grant-makers, let alone face-to-face meetings, quite intimidating. This is not at all uncommon, and is most likely down to a perception relating to the balance of power between your two organisations. Recognising this, and adopting some useful little techniques, can go a long way to overcoming any reluctance to make that call.

Power balance

If you imagine a pair of weighing scales, our perception of the power balance between ourselves (the fundraiser) and the funder (the organisation with the funds) often lies with us being light on one side, and a heavy weight pulling down on the side of the funder (see figure 5.1). We tend to carry the notion that we are trying to sell something and that the grant-maker is the one we are trying to convince to make the purchase.

FIGURE 5.1 Power balance: perception versus reality when approaching funders

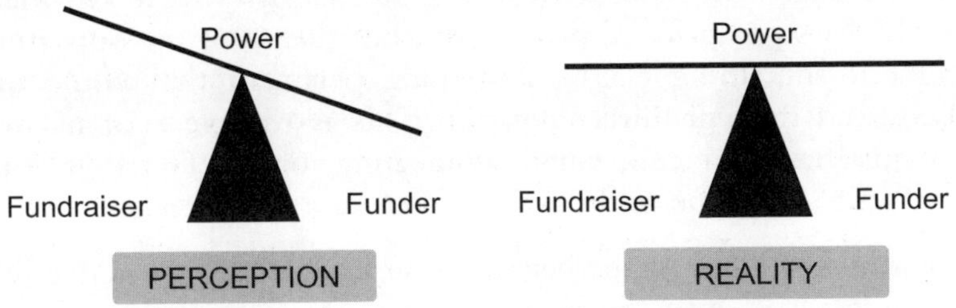

This is not totally wrong. Certainly, we are working to persuade funders of our worthiness as recipients of their money, and indeed much of what is written in this book is about exactly that. We want to engage, inspire and ultimately influence funders to make grants towards our work. The problem comes when we forget the other side of the coin: grant-makers also need grantees. Grant-makers have their own aims and objectives, which are fulfilled through organisations such as yours. Your work can enable them to achieve their goals, just as much as their work can enable you to achieve yours. This mutual benefit is all about partnership, which is what you are looking to develop – rather than begging for a handout. Of course, we are incredibly thankful when we do receive a grant (chapter 8 looks closely at thanking funders), but keeping this level-partnership approach is important during funder engagement.

We can even take this a step further by remembering that for many funders – particularly family foundations, where a grant involves people giving away their own or their family's money – grant-making can feel really good. Even the most formal institutional funders, seemingly with a primary interest in facts and figures and cost-to-income ratio analysis, will be genuinely pleased when their strategic grants programme improves the lives of your beneficiaries. That is what you are working to enable. Remembering this can be a good antidote to pre-meeting nerves or telephone jitters.

The three routes to rapport

A good strategy for engagement, whether at a pre-arranged meeting or if you find yourself in front of a funder at a conference or such, is to enlist some useful tools for initiating and connecting with the funder's key individual.

Bill Bruty, founder and director of Fundraising Training Ltd, created a three-stage technique for successfully engaging with funders during a phone call, face-to-face meeting or even email exchange.[2] It aims to shape the approach to conversations with key individuals, making the first contact effective and memorable, and creating the base of a strong relationship. Here are Bruty's three stages for building rapport:

1. **Fact-finding.** The fundraiser shares and clarifies their knowledge of the funder's policies and procedures, but then uses the opportunity to find out something else – something pertinent that could only be discovered through direct contact. This is the piece of information that justifies your call, email or meeting, or the fact that you have gone up to someone in the coffee queue at a conference.

2. **Empathy-building.** At the beginning of a dialogue, use active listening to put yourself into the other person's shoes and show you understand their perspective. What you say at this stage should reflect what you imagine the funder may be feeling, based on any cues you have picked up from their words or body language. The goal is to get the other person to open up, respond with the emotive part of their brain rather than the factual, and reveal something about themselves.

3. **Connection.** Following on from the empathy that has just been set up, find common ground, such as a shared interest or experience. Exchanging your knowledge about this connection aims to strengthen the bond and make yourself and your organisation memorable to the individual.

Most friendly exchanges between strangers will naturally follow this route, but it can be very useful to keep the three phases in mind if you feel that a conversation is halting or it is difficult to get it going. Once the common ground in the connection part has been established, most people will begin to take down any barriers and be more open to discussion about other matters.

As an example, if a fundraiser were at a conference and they found the opportunity to speak to the key trustee of a prospective grant-maker, a conversation using the three routes to rapport could look something like the following.

Using the three routes in practice

Fundraiser: Hello, Mr Smith, I'm delighted to meet you. My name is Neela Jane and I'm from the Do-Gooder Charity. I really enjoyed your talk. I hadn't realised that you also funded projects in South America, or is it just in Peru exclusively? **[fact-finding]**

Mr Smith: We will consider projects more widely across South America, but we have a preference for Peru due to our founder's historical connections there.

Fundraiser: That's so helpful, thank you. I appreciate your time – I imagine you've been overwhelmed with fundraisers coming up to you all day today. **[empathy]**

Mr Smith: Yes, it has been quite a long day.

Fundraiser: Yes, I'm sure you're looking forward to getting home. **[empathy]** I hope the trains aren't delayed tonight. My youngest is two and won't go to sleep unless I'm there.

Mr Smith: Oh yes, I remember that well. **[connection]**

Fundraiser: Ah, you've been there! How old are your children now?

Mr Smith: They're twelve and nine. They grow up fast – enjoy them while they're little.

Fundraiser: You're absolutely right. They say the days are long but the years are short – it's so true, isn't it? **[empathy/ connection]**

Mr Smith: It is – it's amazing where the time goes when you look back on it.

Fundraiser: Yes, I am really finding that too. Thank you so much, and again for your excellent talk. I hope you won't mind if we keep in touch. Could I give you my card?

Note that in this brief exchange, the vast majority of the conversation is irrelevant to my purpose for speaking with Mr Smith. Instead, we have found a personal common ground that enables us to connect as two humans rather than the representatives of two organisations. This is what builds the initial rapport that will hopefully lead to a warmer professional relationship.

In reality, you might not move through each of the three stages so rapidly and in such a short exchange as in this example. However, keeping these three elements in mind is a useful way of breaking down the initial barrier you may feel when you first meet a funder. If you'd had a conversation along the lines of the above with Mr Smith, it would also have provided an edge when following up with him later. For example, you could have left a message with his assistant or written an email including the words 'I'm the one with the non-sleeping two-year-old', so that he remembered the conversation and would be more likely to respond with warmth.

The key with the three routes to rapport is to keep it as natural as possible, rather than creating a contrived conversation. Even if someone appears not to be forthcoming with any common ground, it is still worth offering a few best-guess clues about yourself (such as family, pets, travel or sporting interests) that can be dropped into conversation and may spark that shared connection.

'But grant-makers don't like events'

If ever a nonsense phrase were regularly banded around, it would be this one. For some reason, there is often a rumble in grants fundraising about the use of events being more suitable for major donor prospects than for the trustees of grant-making organisations. Perhaps the general consensus is that grant-makers, and the people involved in running them, are too busy and important (or stuffy and boring) to want to attend events, and especially anything remotely glamorous in case it seems frivolous. But this simply is not true.

Events are a fantastic way of meeting with prospective funders, including the very formal ones. If they don't want to come, they won't. But, just as with face-to-face meetings, you'll never know if you don't invite them. And the environment of an event can break down barriers with the most unlikely funder.

Events that you might invite a grant-maker to could include lunches, dinners, galas and such – many of which your charity may already be holding. As with a meeting, use the results of your research (see chapter 3) to ascertain who at the funder is the best person to invite, who you really want to meet and engage with, and who is the best person to invite them. You may also wish to put on an event with a specific funder in mind. Roundtables, where experts and people interested in a particular topic come together to discuss certain issues, are an excellent way of engaging with grant-makers. An organisation that is fundraising for a project focused on the preservation of tigers, for example, might host a round-table event where a selection of invited guests come together to hear from the organisation's programme team and discuss the current problem and its potential solutions. The invitees might be conservation experts, academics and funders with an interest in the area. Such events have a triple goal: to promote the important issue generally (which is likely to be an organisational priority); to increase your organisation's reputation as a thought leader in the area; and of course to give you the opportunity to get in front of funders in a way that engages them with your cause.

> We invited the trustees of a very formal trust to our charity's annual gala event. There were celebrities, photographers and an auction for a day on someone's yacht – very glitz and glam, and probably the opposite of what you'd think of for this trust. We invited them anyway, as they were an important prospect. To my surprise, the chair of trustees replied swiftly – it turned out his wife was a big fan of the host of the event, a celebrity chef. They really enjoyed the evening and were much easier to talk to in that kind of environment. It felt like a turning point, which made subsequent conversations easier because we'd built up a bit of a relationship.
>
> **Trust fundraiser**

> Events are very important for face-to-face engagement with grant-makers, as well as providing the opportunity to introduce them to other charity colleagues, particularly your senior leadership. We have found that the type of event is important: grant-makers may be more drawn to an event if it's focused on their core priority areas or where the event is a roundtable where the grant-maker can have their say, instead of simply being talked at. The time of day it takes place is also important. Some grant-makers prefer breakfast events before they go into their office for work, or they may prefer evening events after their work commitments are complete. Finding the right balance and thinking creatively is important to make the event appealing.
>
> Ryan Wilkinson, Head of Foundation Partnerships, UNICEF UK

Conferences and sector-specific events, particularly where a funder may be speaking, are always worth seeking out and attending. Many grant-makers, particularly trusts and foundations as well as institutional and statutory funders, regularly take part in talks and debates about issues related to their priorities. Keep an eye out for relevant events and discussions that are happening and check whether your prospect is speaking or attending. Such events will give you a chance to listen and learn more about your prospect and also provide an opportunity to bring yourself and your organisation to the funder's attention. This can be tricky, especially if there is a long line of other charity representatives waiting to introduce themselves, but persevere – it can't hurt to say hello and that you appreciated their talk, and if you keep your eyes peeled you may be able to introduce yourself at a quieter time. (I once even had a good chat with a prospect at a conference at the sinks in the ladies' loo!) Of course, we need to be mindful of not collaring someone when they want to be left alone (such as on their train journey home or when they are trying to eat their lunch in peace – someone avoiding your eye contact is probably a sign that it's not a good time), but look out for opportunities when the situation seems appropriate.

The key to any event engagement is the follow-up. If someone from the funder's organisation comes to a dinner, send a note (perhaps from your percussionist or lead violinist; see page 63) thanking them for their attendance and personalise it to mention any specifics from your conversation. Use this as an opportunity to get a follow-up meeting, if appropriate, where you can then begin the discussion around your planned funding proposal.

It is also worth thinking of any influential people who could be appropriate event invitees. Trust managers at solicitors' firms, accountants and wealth management companies, for example, often deal with numerous charitable trusts and foundations. While they may not be the key decision-makers themselves, they are likely to hold significant influence. It is worth trying to meet and nurture such people more generally, as the warmer they are to you and the closer they become to your organisation, the more likely they are to mention you when new clients come along and ask for their advice about which charities to support.

Preparing for funder meetings

I vividly remember a funder meeting which did not go well, due to having both over-prepared and under-prepared. It was a family foundation and I had secured a meeting with the key trustee, the settlor whom the foundation was named after. I'd spent the preceding months building a good relationship with his personal assistant and managed to get a rare slot in his diary to come and talk about my organisation's work. I'd done my research and made a plan, so off I trotted along with the programme manager of the project, feeling pretty confident. Until we sat down in the meeting room with him… and his head of corporate relations. While I knew he also owned a company, I thought it was obvious we were there to talk about his personal philanthropy through his family foundation. He thought we were going to discuss potential corporate sponsorship. I had brought the wrong person and the wrong pitch with me, which I delivered anyway while feeling increasingly uncomfortable as he looked uninterested and unimpressed. We tried to follow up afterwards, introducing colleagues from our corporate team and trying to salvage the opportunity, but even my good relationship with his assistant couldn't save the day: they never met with us again and they never gave, from either the foundation or the company.

In this example, which still makes me squirm to recall, I had made assumptions which meant I ended up barking up the wrong tree. If I had simply clarified the purpose of the meeting in advance, I could have saved everyone's time and discomfort, and possibly secured a different kind of support than I originally planned to request.

The purpose of a meeting should never be a surprise to anyone in the room, especially if you are planning to ask for funding face to face. If your intention is to have an initial exploratory conversation, be clear about what you intend when arranging the meeting and clarify that you are not going to be putting a funding proposal to the grant-maker at this stage. Similarly, if you are planning to hand over a proposal during the meeting, make sure your contact is expecting it and is not caught off guard.

If possible, holding an initial exploratory meeting is better than jumping in with your proposal straight away, for two reasons. Firstly, like in my embarrassing story above, you might have a clear idea of a good project fit that is not at all what the funder actually wants to support. An initial meeting helps to work that out through discussion, tests the water, and gives you information to help you tweak and tailor your proposal so that it contains any specific things the grant-maker wants to see detailed. Secondly, it's a bit off-putting meeting someone for the first time and instantly being asked for money. This stage is all about relationship-*building*, prior to the actual ask, so that your contact already knows and hopefully likes and respects your organisation before the proposal even lands on their desk.

The story above also highlights how there needs to be a level of flexibility when you go into a meeting with a funder, as you may have different agendas. For example, you might go in expecting to talk about the equipment needs at a hospice and come out with a new proposition in mind for the salary of a staff nurse, because the conversation revealed a personal link with a key trustee's experience. Be flexible and open-minded.

Conversely, you might find yourself offered a cheque at your first meeting. The funder may assume you are coming to ask for money and kindly offer you a small sum at the very outset. Some like to call this a 'go-away cheque', and if you aren't at the right point in the relationship – the funder doesn't really know much about you yet and isn't yet at all emotionally embedded or connected to your work – it is actually better to

> I once went into a funder meeting where I expected to talk about a particular project and came away with an event venue: it turned out that the charitable trust was fully committed for the foreseeable future, but the trustees were delighted to offer their beautiful home for a high-value fundraising dinner to attract other supporters instead.
>
> **Grants fundraiser**

respectfully decline the funding. Be gracious and grateful, but explain that while the offer is extremely generous, you would like the funder to get to know your organisation's work more first. You are likely to find that a future grant is significantly larger than what was written on that initial cheque.

Increasing your funder engagement

One of the most effective ways of getting in front of funders more is to change your internal focus. Key performance indicators (KPIs) work as well for sole fundraisers as for those in a team. They involve setting monthly targets for various types of activity. These soft targets are set for your own benefit and are different from the hard income targets you may set at an organisational level. They are a motivational tool that should challenge how much time and energy you put into your funder engagement activities and, in turn, prompt you to increase the frequency of these activities and thus the odds of succeeding at the proposal stage.

Typical monthly engagement KPIs could be:

- the number of telephone calls made to prospective or current funders;
- the number of funder meetings or project visits asked for;
- the number of funder meetings or project visits attended;
- the number of peer-to-peer connections used (such as introductions to funders);
- the number of event invitations sent out;
- the number of networking events attended (such as conferences with funders).

You might begin by simply monitoring your existing progress in these areas and then apply some soft targets to increase the frequency of your activities over time. This may initially seem quite dogmatic, but the purpose of tracking these activities is to get a sense of how much you (and your team if relevant) are focusing on the main activities that build funder relationships. There may well be other KPIs to track that are more appropriate for your organisation and they do not have to be set in stone, nor something that you or your team report on formally. They are purely there to motivate. Anything that leads to more engagement leads to better relationships, which in turn leads to greater income from grant-makers. A little like the saying 'take care of the pennies and the pounds look after themselves', the principle is that focusing on these activities will naturally result in more money being raised.

You could also include other KPIs that are less directly related to engagement, such as the number of proposals submitted or the number of new prospects identified. It may also be helpful to track stewardship activities (for example, the number of creative stewardship pieces developed – something we will look at in chapter 8; see page 133). Essentially, any activity in your grants fundraising which will ultimately lead to more income is worth monitoring and encouraging.

Spotlight: does a relationship really matter?

It might seem much easier to put an application straight in than to go to the time and effort required for engagement activities. So just how important are relationships to grant-makers, and do they value getting to know us in the same way as we might them?

A paper by the Council for Advancement and Support of Education examined key empirical studies from psychology, sociology and economics to explore how the science of philanthropy can inform fundraising activity.[3] Based on this research, the report proposes a 'DIME' model for fundraising strategy, which considers donation impact, motivation and effort:

- **Donation impact.** Research backs up the idea that funders want to know their support is going to make a real difference and that their actions matter. The more tangible the impact they are shown, the more powerful the effect, with one study finding that funders which felt a greater sense of specific impact gave nearly twice as much as those that received general impact information.[4]

- **Motivation.** Research also shows that understanding funder motivation – why someone gives, and in a certain way – is a critical component of pitching the funding proposition and framing appeals in a way that aligns with a funder's core values, goals and motivations. Evidence has specifically highlighted that framing the ask according to a funder's motivations for either agency (what an individual funder can do to make a difference) or communion (what we can all do together to make a change) may increase how much is given – but not when the ask is framed to address both of these possible motivations.[5] Therefore, understanding which is the greater motivating factor can affect how you approach a funder and how much you later receive.

- **Effort.** Data further shows that funders prefer to put some form of effort into the process of giving and into their involvement in the fundraising process, as this enables their giving to be more meaningful.[6] This is converse to the perception that any effort required on the funder's part is inconvenient and off-putting; rather, research suggests that greater involvement and engagement are more likely to result in significant and long-term giving.

Activities such as meetings, events and project visits serve to address the three elements of the DIME model: such engagement enables funders to fully understand the *impact* of your work and therefore of any potential grants; it grows your understanding of the funders' *motivations* as you get to know them better, in order to frame the proposition in the most effective way; and it allows funders to have a level of *effortful* involvement in the process, which is more meaningful. As the research shows, these factors in turn increase your likelihood of success at the proposal stage.

Two trustees share why they appreciate grant-seekers engaging with them before submitting proposals:

> It was during the time I was the administrator, as well as a trustee, for the Edith Murphy Foundation that I realised how very important it was to build relationships with the charities we were funding. Once the relationship had begun, usually some or all of the trustees became involved with the relationship as it developed. There is no doubt that events, meetings, project visits and the like cement those relationships, as they provide a forum for interaction and the opportunity to meet representatives face to face. During the COVID-19 pandemic, things have had to be different. Many charities provided information through online presentations and interactive involvement has sometimes been possible in this way. However, while online involvement has been invaluable, I do not believe it can replace the personal interaction provided by face-to-face meetings.
>
> Richard Adkinson, Trustee at the
> Edith Murphy Foundation

> As a trustee of numerous family trusts, I have experienced first hand the necessity of getting to know the charities we choose to support. Invitations to events and meetings with fundraisers and charity staff help to grow our understanding of the workings and priorities of an organisation. These are the insights that inform whether we will go on to fund a project and, if so, at what level. Rather than a waste of a charity's time or resources, such relationship development opportunities are a sensible investment. Likewise, fundraisers should seek to get to know us as grant-makers, so that an application and the ensuing relationship is managed in the most appropriate way.
>
> Charles Hicks, Private Client Solicitor
> and Partner at Wedlake Bell LLP

Conclusion

Relationships are the core of any grants fundraising strategy. Prioritising engagement is just as important for formal, institutional grant-makers as it is for family foundations, as it focuses on forming strong connections that are relevant across all funder types. Meetings, events and phone calls are all simple but effective ways of increasing interpersonal interaction, and they are appreciated more by funders than we might assume.

In a nutshell...

- Developing a good relationship prior to submitting a proposal is one of the best ways of increasing your chance of funding success – relationships turn into partnerships. Work out who are the best people to engage with, and who from your side should be part of the overall relationship.

- Don't assume that grant-makers will never want to meet with you or attend your event; they definitely won't come if you don't invite them!

- Use your connectors to make introductions and initiate relationships. Remember that the power of a connection can break down the barrier to even the most elusive funder.

- Try not to make assumptions ahead of funder meetings and clarify the purpose. An ask – including handing over a proposal – should never be a surprise and will ideally come after a relationship has been built.

- Remember the power balance. You are not a window salesperson; you have something fantastic to offer funders that could inspire and fulfil their grant-making purposes.

Notes

1 *Funding Social Change: How can grant-seekers and grant-makers collaborate to better serve our communities?* [PDF], KEDA Consulting, 2021, www.kedaconsulting.co.uk/wp-content/uploads/2021/06/keda_consulting_funding_social_change_a4_50pp_V2.pdf, p. 23, accessed 7 December 2021.

2 The three-stage technique is explored as part of training by Fundraising Training Ltd; see www.fundraisingtraining.co.uk.

3 Ashley Whillans, *A Brief Introduction to the Science of Fundraising* [PDF], Council for Advancement and Support of Education, 2016, www.hbs.edu/ris/Publication%20Files/WhitePaper_ac7c4ea5-a635-4338-8d1e-4aa736fbe263_b9a54c18-be5e-4cd8-b166-7442361fb64b.pdf, accessed 7 December 2021.

4 Cynthia Cryder, George Loewenstein and Richard Scheines, 'The Donor is in the Details', *Organizational Behaviour and Human Decision Processes*, vol. 120, no. 1, 2013, pp. 15–23.

5 Ashley Whillans and Elizabeth Dunn, 'Agentic Appeals Increase Charitable Giving in an Affluent Sample of Donors', *PLOS One*, 2018, https://doi.org/10.1371/journal.pone.0208392.

6 Christopher Olivola and Eldar Shafir, 'The Martyrdom Effect: When pain and effort increase prosocial contributions', *Journal of Behavioural Decision Making*, vol. 26, no. 1, 2013, pp. 90–105.

CHAPTER SIX

Developing the proposal

Introduction

If the previous chapters made up the bottom layer of our sponge cake model (see figure 1.2), we have now reached the jam – the rich, sweet filling in between the two other layers (getting to know a funder and then – hopefully – getting to thank them). The proposal itself is a critical document, with success often hinging on its quality and content. Developing this document is, much like fundraising in general, both an art and a science. You will need to be persuasive, inspiring, even emotionally engaging at times, while also including all the necessary components for a comprehensive description of your project.

Written proposals can take several forms. Some grant-makers have application forms, varying in length and detail, which may be on paper or online. Institutional and statutory funders in particular often have several proposal stages, sometimes starting with an initial expression of interest (often just EOI). Others will leave it up to you to present your proposal as you like. In such cases, bear in mind that a standard proposal is ideally no more than two sides of A4, unless stated otherwise by the grant-maker or if it is for a particularly large grant that warrants a lot of detail.

This chapter will use the term 'project' to describe what you are seeking funds for, but this could be a distinct project, a wider programme or general funds. Whatever the type of funding, the way you present the proposition to a funder will be much the same, including particular core elements to describe the work. We will explore each of these, which together should provide your funders with a complete and engaging picture of the work you want them to support.

Key components

Whether freestyle, with no specified format, or an application form with particular questions, any funding proposal should aim to address nine key components. As highlighted on page 90, these components broadly fall into three categories: the overarching context, the delivery of the project and the details of the money involved. These, in turn, reflect the main aims of any kind of proposal: communicating the importance of the need, your effectiveness in meeting that need and the cost-effectiveness of your approach.

The context	**Title and executive summary:** the overview **The problem:** the need **The solution:** what you will do about it
The operation	**User involvement:** your beneficiaries' input and insight **Monitoring and evaluation:** how you will know you've been successful **Dissemination:** how you will share the results, findings and lessons
The money	**Sustainability:** how the work will continue **Budget:** how much you need to do it **The ask:** your request

It is important to note that the level of detail you present for each component will vary hugely from funder to funder. Some grant-makers will have more of a focus on sustainability, for example, and therefore a proposal to such a funder will need to give more attention to that area. Others, such as the National Lottery Community Fund, place particular emphasis on user involvement, which other funders may be less concerned with. For this reason, while it is very helpful to have your project information pre-prepared, it is best practice to write the proposal itself from scratch with a specific funder in mind and not to re-hash or tweak an already written version.

Note also that you don't necessarily need to use these particular headings. Depending on the project you are presenting, the funder it is for and the amount of space you have (for example, the funder may require a maximum word count or number of pages), sections may be merged together or overlapped. Indeed, some funders may require you to use their own chosen headings or subheadings. Either way, the *content* is the main thing, as these are the core areas that funders commonly expect to see described. Let's explore each one in turn.

The context

Title and executive summary (or 'Who are this lot and what are they after?')

A short title, summarising your project in one phrase, is the first thing the recipient will read and probably the last thing you should write. Once you have a complete picture of what you are asking for, give your proposal a title that is instantly engaging and that captures the essence of the project. For example, returning to the Hedgehog Rescue Association from chapter 4, if you were writing a proposal for the bonfire rescue project, you might give it the title 'Protecting the Great British Hedgehog' or something similarly (or more) catchy.

In a freestyle proposal, the first section is then the executive summary. This is a bit like an elevator pitch, presenting the gist of the whole proposal in a short paragraph. Keep it clear and concise, describing what your organisation is all about and what you do, the scope of the project and what specifically you are asking for. If yours is a well-known organisation, a couple of sentences may suffice as introduction. Other charities may need to provide a little more information, including your overall vision and mission, the basic essence of your work, any interesting facts about when or how your organisation was started, and any significant accomplishments that show your credibility (such as from your fact-file; see page 57). The reader will want to understand what your unique selling points are – that is, what is special or different about your work or approach, compared to those of others in your field? Or, are you the only charity that does what you do?

Many grant-makers have an initial sift of all the proposals they have received. In this case, someone from the funder's team may read and summarise your proposal, and, if it is deemed eligible, then the funder's main decision-makers will use that summary as a basis to form their grants decision. Make the funder's job easier by summarising your proposal for them in your executive summary to capture the key points of your project's objectives, outputs and outcomes (which we'll explore below; see page 93) and the precise request you are making of the funder.

Aim to answer the following questions in your executive summary:

- What is your organisation all about and what makes it special?
- What shows that you are effective, and what are your strengths?
- What do you currently do?
- What do you want to do?
- Why is this project important?
- What do you need to enable you to do it?
- How can this funder help you?
- How would this fit in with the funder's own interests or objectives?

The problem (or 'What's the issue?')

On page 58, we looked at how to find evidence of the need that your work addresses. This is the part of the proposal where you should present this need, and the evidence for it, in a convincing and also hopeful way. You need to show that the issue is significant but that the situation should and can be changed.

The secret to describing the problem well is to focus entirely on the impact upon your beneficiary group, which is what funders are most interested in. This means describing what a particular problem means for your beneficiaries, rather than talking about your organisation's immediate need or even the service itself. For instance, if a youth centre needs a new roof, it is much more powerful to talk about why the roof needs to be fixed (to enable the young people using the youth centre to do A, B and C, which is important because of X, Y and Z) than to focus on describing the holes and the fact that water is leaking in. Frame the problem, and therefore the basis of your whole proposal, around the difference you want to see in the lives of your beneficiaries.

Of course, some needs are simply more popular and easier to 'sell' than others. Causes that are less known about or that are generally misunderstood – such as certain health conditions that receive inadequate attention, or socially stigmatised beneficiary groups – may seem more challenging in terms of raising funds. However, you can turn this into an advantage by highlighting these facts and using statistical evidence to show how a need is under-funded and therefore particularly warrants support. Grant-makers often favour causes that are otherwise overlooked, particularly if a grant could make a huge impact or a project might not happen at all without it. They won't want to replace funding that could easily be found elsewhere, so play to this strength; yours could be the cause through which they make that particularly significant difference.

> Articulating need is fundamental to any fundraising ask. It enables you to make an emotional connection with the reader and to more clearly demonstrate the impact that your work will have. Our top tips would be to balance statistics and data with real stories and quotes, make it relatable to the reader, and demonstrate the urgency.
>
> Victoria Ives, Trusts and Statutory Manager, St John Ambulance

Using your collated evidence (i.e. the facts and figures to back up how you know this is an issue), this section of your proposal should answer the following questions:

- **What impact does this problem have on your beneficiaries?** Describe why this issue is important and be clear about who or what it affects (your beneficiary group). Be careful not to assume that everyone already knows it is a problem.
- **What is the urgency?** Why does it need to be addressed now?
- **What will happen if nothing is done?** State the consequences of no action being taken, such as the situation worsening as the problem becomes more acute or the knock-on economic impact of not addressing the issue.
- **Are you looking to prevent something?** Prevention is usually preferable to (and cheaper than) a cure, so emphasise the point if your project will involve preventative work.

- **Are there specifics of the area or community that make this issue particularly pertinent?** Where possible, use statistics to show the prevalence of the problem in the location or community you are working in.

The solution (or 'What are they doing about it?')

Once the reader understands the scope and scale of the problem, you need to show them a clear plan for how your work will address it. Many application forms will explicitly ask you to describe the three Os: your objectives, outcomes and outputs (see figure 6.1). Some will also ask what your inputs are. Whether in a freestyle proposal or a form, it is important to dissect these elements in order to explain to the funder what exactly your project will do.

FIGURE 6.1 Objectives, outcomes, outputs and inputs

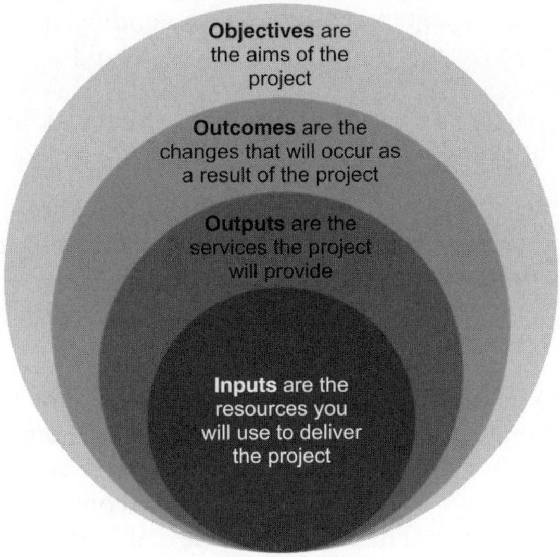

Using our project to rescue hedgehogs on Guy Fawkes Night, these elements might look as follows:

- **The objective:** to prevent hedgehogs getting stuck in bonfires.
- **The outcome:** increased numbers of protected hedgehogs and the survival of a vulnerable species.
- **The output:** our bonfire checking service.
- **The input:** a wildlife protection officer, the salary for whom we are seeking funds.

It's not always easy to work out your three Os, particularly for more complex or layered projects. NCVO Charities Evaluation Services has a very helpful Planning Triangle (available on its website at https://knowhow.ncvo.org.uk/how-to/copy_of_how-to-create-a-planning-triangle), which can help you to identify the three Os for your particular project.

Grant-makers commonly place a strong emphasis on outcomes in their priorities, looking for both short- and long-term impacts of their funding.[1] Therefore, while you will be looking for funding for your desired inputs, it is the outcomes (and ultimately objectives) that you will need to talk about the most – the funder will be supporting the central layer in order to achieve the two outermost layers of figure 6.1, so these outermost layers are where you should focus your proposal.

Funders usually require both objectives and outcomes to be SMART, that is:

- **specific:** tightly defined and relating directly to the identified need;
- **measurable:** progress can be measured at the start, during and at the end of the project;
- **achievable:** sufficient capacity and resources (financial, human and material) to do the work;
- **realistic:** capable of being achieved with the specified resources and within the agreed timescale (some funders use 'relevant' instead, meaning having a strong connection to their priorities);
- **timebound:** set within a specific time frame.

Note that some funders have their own specific outcome priorities and may wish to see your project closely align with those. Frame your outcomes to be as relevant to theirs as possible, taking note of the type of language they use to present them, but be aware that your outcomes must be internally defined first rather than designed around those of a funder (see page 150).

As well as describing the three Os clearly, this section of your proposal should answer the following questions:

- **How will the project's outcomes meet the identified need?** Explain how the project's outcomes will make a difference (not simply state that they will) and explain why this is the best way to sufficiently address the problem. For instance, why is a dedicated wildlife protection officer the best method of addressing the issue of hedgehogs getting stuck in bonfires?
- **Where, when and who?** Describe where the project will take place and why that is the case – does the geographical location have any specific features that make it particularly important for the project (for example, do more bonfires take place there)? What is the start date and the time

frame for completion of the project – how long will it take? Who are you specifically aiming to work with in terms of any service delivery partners, and how many beneficiaries will the project reach (i.e. how many hedgehogs are you aiming to rescue)?

- **How will this fit with other, related work?** Perhaps the project will build on previous activities or supplement existing provision by another organisation. Describe any relevant links or collaboration with any other agencies doing similar work, and how this project will complement rather than duplicate others' activities. This is also an opportunity to show why and how your organisation is perfectly placed to address this particular issue.

- **What is fresh, interesting or innovative about your approach?** You should aim to excite the funder by describing the project, or pulling out elements of it, as offering something that is original and that captures the imagination. Even for a straightforward intervention, you will ideally want the reader to think 'That is brilliant – how have we not thought of this before?'

- **What is the project's theory of change?** Some funders, particularly larger and more institutional ones, will be explicitly interested in the theory of change behind your project. This is the explanation of how and why your project aims to bring about the changes proposed, and the trajectory of outcomes that is required to achieve your desired impact. For a comprehensive description of your theory of change, you might choose to include graphics such as flow charts and diagrams, although these are only mandatory if stipulated by the funder. NCVO has a very helpful description and templates for how to build a theory of change: https://knowhow.ncvo.org.uk/how-to/how-to-build-a-theory-of-change.

Note that for this section of the proposal, you will want to focus in particular on any activities you are specifically requesting funding towards. For example, if you were asking for support to fund your wildlife protection officer, you would want to outline any specifics about this role as well as describing the overall project.

> The issues we're focused on are often structural and systemic – but they're not impossible to overcome. We're looking for organisations that understand that. They can bring dynamism to the challenges and direct experience of the issues. And, as a result, they aren't afraid to challenge the status quo and give a fresh perspective on how to address long-held problems. We want to see a real honesty about what it's going to take to tackle the issue. That includes not doing it all alone and asking themselves questions about who else is key to making this happen – and how we can work with them to do it.
>
> Hannah Lim, Funding Manager, Esmée Fairbairn Foundation

The operation

User involvement (or 'Who have they consulted?')

Grant-makers increasingly want to see that your beneficiaries have been actively consulted and involved in the development of your project. Institutional funders, in particular, are often especially interested in user involvement. This needs to be a genuine, significant input into the planning process and not just a token consultation to tick a box.

The point of user involvement is to demonstrate that you haven't just assumed that you know what is best for your beneficiary group. You will need to show that your project will address real needs in a way that is going to be effective and actually used by your beneficiaries, and that you have the support and commitment of those for whom you are working.

> We usually ask applicants to show how the people who would benefit from the grant have influenced the plans for the project, as well as how they will continue to be involved in the delivery if the project is funded. Grant applicants can demonstrate this in a broad range of ways, such as: day-to-day chats with those who currently benefit from services being delivered and with other interested people in the community; holding stalls at local events; engaging people through, say, coffee mornings or online questionnaires; visiting local community groups; and so on. We want to understand how the wider community is engaged with the idea.
>
> Andrew Owen, Head of Funding Wales,
> The National Lottery Community Fund

Ways of engaging your beneficiaries with your project can include:

- **Involving beneficiaries in running your organisation.** If appropriate to your cause, including beneficiaries among your trustee board, paid staff or volunteers is hugely valuable and reflective of why your organisation exists. Of course, if your beneficiaries are hedgehogs, this might need to be a little less direct. But including people who are closely connected to your beneficiary group provides knowledge and sympathy, which will be important to both your organisation's management and funders.

- **Involving beneficiaries in shaping your project plans.** You can do this using beneficiary group consultations, questionnaires, community surveys and such like. You can also seek beneficiaries' feedback in the monitoring and evaluation process (described on page 97).

- **Involving beneficiaries in running the project itself.** Volunteer roles and roles as part of the project steering group are good ways of ensuring beneficiaries have input into the project's delivery and are fully on board with the ideas being put forward.

- **Involving beneficiaries in fundraising for the project,** if and where appropriate. This also helps to demonstrate how much beneficiaries truly value the project and wish for it to go ahead or continue.

Another way the experience of beneficiaries will be relevant to your proposal is through case study material, such as quotes and photographs. These can really bring to life your description of the need and the impact of your work.

Monitoring and evaluation (or 'How do they know it will work?')

Most grant-makers place great value on monitoring and evaluation. Some major funders have entire departments dedicated purely to this one area, which involves monitoring and evaluating the effectiveness of their grants and the work of their grantees. In essence, this is all about providing evidence that what you are doing is making a difference. You will remember that funders want your objectives and outcomes to be SMART (see page 94). As the second letter in the acronym highlights, they need to be measurable so that you – and your funder – can assess progress against them.

It is important to understand the distinction between these terms: monitoring is about gaining information, whereas evaluation is about the decisions made in light of this information. This section of your proposal aims to show funders how you plan to carry out monitoring and evaluation for your project, so you know that it is achieving what you set out to achieve.

Monitoring involves tracking and reporting against specific and measurable indicators (such as targets or milestones), which you should have identified at the early stages of planning your project and which should reflect the results that you expect to see. Indicators can be both quantitative (for example, the number of hedgehogs you anticipate will be rescued) and qualitative (such as feedback from people involved in the project, gathered through a survey), and they should be linked directly to the outcomes and outputs already outlined in your proposal. Some funders may also want to see a description of how you plan to gather this information. The important thing is that your monitoring processes must make it clear whether or not the outcomes have been achieved. For more detail on how to measure outcomes and indicators, see NCVO's guidance (https://knowhow.ncvo.org.uk/how-to/how-to-develop-a-monitoring-and-evaluation-framework).

Funders may also want to understand what you plan to do in terms of evaluation – how you plan to use the monitoring information to improve your project along the way and inform any further development of the work. Evaluation can take the form of a brief statement of what was achieved with a grant, an in-depth report of measurable objectives, or anything in between. However, it must be very much about action – how you will make appropriate changes and adjustments as the work proceeds, and how you will demonstrate your project's effectiveness. A well-designed project will have evaluation built into it from the start, so that feedback is received at every stage (an added benefit is that this is likely to be cheaper than doing a separate evaluation at the end). It should also be independent and professional, carried out by a credible person or organisation such as a consultancy (where budgets permit and where relevant to the project).

As well as involving your beneficiaries in the early development of the project, it is important that you don't leave them out of the monitoring or the evaluation. As part of this, you should take seriously any comments or feedback received as part of the process, and users should also be involved in the ongoing development of the project in addition to the initial design. For very large proposals, it is worthwhile setting up a small steering group to give input on the monitoring and evaluation activities, and how to describe them in the proposal. This group should include the main stakeholders in the project, such as key and senior staff at your organisation and any partner organisations and, crucially, users.

Not all funders will require the same level of detail for this section of a proposal, or indeed the same type of information. For some, it will suffice to include a few brief sentences to show that you are doing some form of monitoring and evaluation. For others (usually the larger and more institutional or statutory funders), more description of the planned monitoring and evaluation tools and systems will be required. Whether it is brief or detailed, the overall aim of this section is to reassure the funder that the project is well thought out and that you have a clear basis for measuring its success.

Dissemination (or 'What happens next?')

As well as knowing that a project will be carefully measured for its effectiveness, a grant-maker may wish to know how you will make further use of the outcomes you have identified. This is dissemination: the spread of information and ideas. With our hedgehogs, for example, we may do a wonderful job looking through bonfires and rescuing any spiny friends trapped inside for the duration of our project, but what happens next? Funders will want to know that your work won't just come to an abrupt halt when their funding is up. They will want to see that there are plans in place for how any relevant results, findings and lessons will be used beyond the project itself.

As part of your dissemination, you might plan to feed out the knowledge you have gained about ongoing needs into your wider organisation as well as externally to inform other work. Your main aim when talking about this area should be to show the wider impact of your project, demonstrate how you will share lessons learned with others, and promote best practice to be replicated elsewhere, long after the grant has been spent.

It is worth noting here that 'impact' is a bit of a buzzword in fundraising. Of course, grant-makers want to know that their grants are impactful, so you do need to describe your intended impact in terms of both the project itself and your wider dissemination efforts. However, it is important to remember that funders are equally interested in vision. This means that while you should be enthusiastic about what you plan to achieve from this specific project, you must include just as much information about where you are heading long term: your future goals and how you are going to get there. This vision is ultimately what a funder is looking to invest in and become a part of.

For some projects and some funders, dissemination can be a very important part of a grant and requires a full costing and separate line in the budget. A proposal for a research project, for instance, will need to describe how research findings will be shared and communicated. For a publication, as another example, the proposal may need to talk about how the end product will be distributed locally, nationally or beyond. As with monitoring and evaluation, some (usually larger) funders will require detailed descriptions of dissemination plans within the proposal. For others, you could touch upon monitoring and evaluation, dissemination and sustainability (the topic of the next section) more lightly, and tie them together into one section.

The money

Sustainability (or 'Does it all end with us?')

Similarly to dissemination, sustainability looks beyond the grant and what happens at the end of the initial project. Funders will want to know that you have plans in place to either continue or build upon the work they have funded. Few funders are interested in short-term solutions to problems – sticking a plaster on an issue. This is the section where you describe how your organisation's planning will ensure either that the grant will be replaced with funds from other sources (for instance, the funding may be for a pilot project that will receive statutory support once proven successful) or that the project will make its own income in the long run.

These last two scenarios illustrate the concept of leverage, where a relatively small investment helps to create a much larger impact. As another example, if our hedgehog rescue project were successfully run in one location, its positive results might lead to a national roll-out. As a result, investing in the initial idea would provide the leverage for a much wider-scale benefit over the longer term – which would be likely to appeal to most funders.

Leverage can also be talked about as part of sustainability if you can demonstrate how a grant would be used to mobilise further funding from elsewhere. Ways of doing this include:

- **Matching grants:** companies use this principle when they offer to match their employees' fundraising pound for pound. The same principle can work for funders, where one may agree to pay half or part of the costs if you can raise the remainder. This is then a compelling ask for other grant-makers, if their grant would essentially unlock funds from another organisation and provide double value for their investment.

- **Development leverage:** this is where the funder invests in the infrastructure of your organisation, which on the surface might not sound very exciting but will actually result in increased income. A grant for a new fundraising database, for example, could enable integration and efficiency, creating significantly greater income for your organisation.

- **Demonstrating cost-effectiveness:** this applies where there are savings resulting from your work that can be assigned a cash value. For example, addressing a particular health need might result in a reduction of medical care costs for the NHS. Or, using our example, the protection of hedgehogs might have a wider environmental impact that supports the local ecosystem. If you can show how there may be a resulting value that is greater than that of the grant, you are particularly demonstrating the power of leverage.

The overarching goal of this section of your proposal is to show that your financial plan for the project is secure and sustainable in both the medium and the long term. Essentially, you need to show that investing in this work is a safe bet.

Unless you are looking for full project funding, this section should also cover any anticipated funding from other sources and your overall fundraising plan for the project. This will put the grant into context and explain where you intend to obtain the balance if other funds are required. You may also wish to mention any other funders that are already on board, with their permission.

> At Trust for London we try to take a balanced approach to sustainability. We encourage organisations we fund to ensure the benefits of projects last as long as possible when our funding ends. But we are also realistic about whether organisations can keep the work going without an additional grant, or produce measurable, sustainable results from one funding round. We prefer not to be an organisation's sole funder, and may check when we do an assessment visit that an organisation has considered other funders and what will happen if an application is unsuccessful. That helps to assess an organisation's capacity around grants fundraising and work planning, and also gives our trustees information to allocate funding between competing applications.
>
> Susie Dye, Grants Manager, Trust for London

Budget (or 'What's all this going to cost?')

By this point in your proposal, you will hopefully have sold the idea of the need and your ability to address it. Remember that this is the aim: selling an idea, rather than asking for money. The budget can feel like a complex part of the proposal; however, while it is a central component, its purpose is simply to break down what this excellent idea is going to cost.

Much like with the other sections, the level of detail a budget requires will depend on the funder. Some will request a specific breakdown, and the size of the financial ask you are making will likely affect how granular you need to be. Regardless of its size, a good budget will include a line-by-line description of the main project expenses. As a general rule, the bigger the project and the bigger the ask, the more detailed the budget will need to be.

One of the main things to bear in mind when working up a budget is that you need to capture what the project will *really* cost. While funders want to be assured that you are taking a cost-effective approach – so it can be tempting to try to make things look as inexpensive as possible – it is also important not to under-budget, as this can be disastrous. Remember the power balance we looked at on page 77 – don't be apologetic because your project costs what it costs. Funders want to know that you are budgeting wisely, but they don't want you to compromise on quality in the hopes of getting a grant and then not be able to deliver the objectives. This means that the budget has to reflect *all* the costs, including any associated costs, of the work as a whole.

Full cost recovery

Even if your proposal is for a specific project or aspect of your work, rather than for unrestricted funding, there will be more than just the direct costs of the project to factor into your budget.

Core costs – or overheads – are your organisation's central expenses and they keep it going; they include the costs of management, IT systems, research and development, and financial planning. While these things might not sound like the most attractive items to present to a funder, they are an essential part of your budget since your project and wider services will become dangerously unsustainable without them. Insufficient core funding results in under-investment in infrastructure, leadership, governance and strategic development – all of which can spell disaster for a charity long term. Factoring all these costs into your budget is therefore incredibly important, and is called full cost recovery (FCR).

The key to FCR is to reframe the way you think about core costs, rather than considering them a separate item that funders don't really want to see. One way to do this is to think of the project as a series of activities, with full overhead costs analysed and legitimately built into each one. Another way is to add up the activity costs and then add an extra percentage, such as 15%, to the subtotal as a separate 'essential costs' line in the budget (pick whatever percentage is realistic for your organisation to cover the relevant core costs, although note that most funders would baulk at more than 15%). Whichever way you do it, the total should reflect the full, necessary costs of the whole project, including all 'hidden' costs, such as training, travel, any publications you need to buy, pension contributions, National Insurance, office space costs (including heating and lighting), postage, staff supervision and so on. If you are using a budget given to you by someone else, such as a programme manager, double-check that adequate overheads have been included for these items either as a separate line or within the various activity lines.

Footnotes can be useful to explain how overheads have been calculated as well as to disclose any funding you have already received for core costs. This is better than not including such information at all and it looking like you have just forgotten about overheads, and it also adds confidence and credibility if you have already received some income.

Most grant-makers are increasingly savvy about the reality and necessity of FCR, seeing it as a true reflection of a project's cost. Many – in particular statutory, institutional and larger trusts and foundations – expect budgets to use the FCR model and recognise that if overheads have not been paid for, then the project is not being fully funded. Others even explicitly support core costs. Examples include Comic Relief and the National Lottery Community Fund, both of which have 'development funding' streams at the time of writing, specifically supporting infrastructure needs to enable organisations to grow and develop.

The other useful aspect of FCR is that funders can be assured that they are paying for the overheads supporting their specific project, rather than subsidising other work. It is, therefore, the most transparent, efficient and accurate way of presenting a budget.

Finally, do also be mindful of inflation costs. You will need to take inflation into account, particularly if the project will be running in another one, two or more years' time; if you are calculating costs based on this or last years' costs; or if the budget is for an ongoing multi-year project.

The ask (or 'What do they want from us?')

The very last section of your proposal is probably the most important: the funding request. It may only be a line, or a few short lines, but it is the pinnacle of the whole document as it outlines what exactly you want the funder to do with all the information you have presented.

With this in mind, be confident, clear and concise. Ask for a specific sum of money, rather than suggesting that 'any contribution will be gratefully received', as the latter looks like you either haven't done your research or don't really know what you need. Specify if the grant is required over a number of years and what exactly the funding is for. If the grant would be a general contribution to the overall budget rather than for a specific item or activity, make sure that this will be obvious to the reader. And if you have any timing restrictions, such as if you require funding by a particular date for the project to run, be sure to state this clearly.

Your ask could be as simple as 'We would like to ask the X Foundation for a grant of X over X years, towards X.' It could also be presented as a shopping list, where the funder has options for different grant levels, such as '£20,000 would support the entire project to run for one year, £10,000 would provide the equipment required for the project, £5,000 would enable the data-collection element of the project to take place' and so forth. However, unless the funder has asked for these different options, it is much better to present a clear and specific request as this shows that you are confident in your needs.

> Don't be afraid to talk about money (so many applicants are!). Tell us what you need, why you need it, and what you will spend it on – being clear and open about finances gives us confidence that any money we give you will make a difference and we both will learn from what goes well and what doesn't.
>
> Caroline Taylor, Chief Executive,
> Essex Community Foundation

Finally, if there would be any benefits for the funder, this is the place to state them. For example, if you are approaching a corporate foundation, you may be offering employee engagement benefits or the opportunity for a grant-maker to have its name on a plaque somewhere. It is appropriate to highlight this within the proposal where it is relevant to the project and where you know, from your research, that it would be a key part of the attraction for the funder.

Spotlight: informational issues

Given the technical nature of developing proposals for grant-makers, fundraisers often rely on the quality and availability of the project information they can glean from internal colleagues. With programme staff often working under pressure, even large organisations can find it challenging to source the types and levels of information that funders require.

Research by KEDA Consulting found that fundraisers face common challenges in developing funding proposals due to internal barriers of this kind. A survey of 248 fundraisers in the UK revealed that:

- Only 40% of fundraisers found it easy to access the information they require to develop funding proposals, such as internal finance, policies, evidence to back up claims in their proposal and information on front-line services.
- Just over half (54%) felt confident that they were taking the best approach with a funder, such as knowing which aspect of their work to apply for funding towards.
- Around 60% felt that there were gaps in the delivery details required for their funding proposals, such as clear objectives, outcomes and outputs, and 40% had gaps in their budget detail or funding plans.
- Some 72% believed they were not able to clearly demonstrate the difference they made or fully show their impact through concrete outcomes and stories of change, using systems to monitor, evaluate, and use learning and insight in their work.[2]

This final figure was consistent across organisations of different sizes, suggesting that this is not just an issue for smaller or new grant-seeking organisations. How can we address these internal issues to get full organisational buy-in and support for grants fundraising, and access to the detail needed to develop the best possible proposals? Two organisations describe how clarifying roles and prioritising communication are key to overcoming these challenges and garnering internal support:

> Many complex proposals and grants are very technical and require a lot of input from programme specialists. Our programme colleagues will have different levels of involvement depending on the size of the grant and the level of technical input and support needed. We have found it important to have agreed roles and responsibilities between the trust fundraiser and programme colleague, so that

everyone is clear on the expectations around managing the proposal development process and any subsequent grant. Regular and clear internal communication is crucial.

Luke Brocket, Head of Private Foundations, UNICEF UK

For any relationship to thrive, there needs to be alignment between values, aspirations and leadership. Institutional buy-in is key for success in developing major asks and building sustained partnerships, both of which should be considered as strategic priorities and must be supported by our senior leaders. We don't have it cracked yet and it is always a work in progress. Fundraising is not a solo sport, and it is important that as a whole team we are working together on successful, long-term funder relationships where all parties respect and care for each other's interests, and the collective difference we can make to lives, society and our planet.

Jhumar Johnson, Chief of Staff to the Vice-Chancellor, The Open University

Conclusion

Proposal development can be a complicated process, as it involves presenting detailed project information across several key components in the way that is most appropriate for a given funder. This means that a one-size-fits-all approach is rarely successful, and proposals should be developed with a funder's specific interests and criteria in mind.

In a nutshell...

- Developing the proposal is the jam layer of our sponge cake model (see figure 1.2) – central, but not stand-alone, and best served between the crucial layers of getting to know and effectively stewarding funder relationships.
- The nine key components of a strong proposal make up the basis of any funder proposition, covering the overall context of your work, the operational details that will support the project, and the financials required to make it happen.
- Ensure that your beneficiaries are an integral part of your organisation's project planning. Funders increasingly want to see genuine user involvement, including in the way that your project is monitored and evaluated.
- Budget carefully, but don't forget about your core costs. Full cost recovery means including – in an accurate and justifiable way – all the elements that will support your project and enable it to run.

• Grant-seekers from organisations of all shapes and sizes can find it a challenge to glean the appropriate level of project information that grant-makers require. Developing strong internal relationships and systems can go a long way towards making this process easier for all involved.

Notes

1 Paula D. Johnson, *Global Philanthropy Report: Perspectives on the global foundation sector* [PDF], The Hauser Institute for Civil Society, 2018, https://cpl.hks.harvard.edu/files/cpl/files/global_philanthropy_report_final_april_2018.pdf, p. 27, accessed 9 February 2022.

2 *Funding Social Change: How can grant-seekers and grant-makers collaborate to better serve our communities?* [PDF], KEDA Consulting, 2021, www.kedaconsulting.co.uk/wp-content/uploads/2021/06/keda_consulting_funding_social_change_a4_50pp_V2.pdf, accessed 7 December 2021.

CHAPTER SEVEN

Submitting the ask

Introduction

The chair of a charitable foundation once described how he didn't open envelopes he received in the post unless they passed the 'pen test': he would lick his finger and smear the ink to see whether the words had been written with a ballpoint pen or fountain pen. The latter went to the trustees' meeting for consideration and the rest went in the bin.

This story might sound extreme and even a little ridiculous but, as well as being true, it highlights that the person on the receiving end of a proposal will have their own preferences, biases and pet peeves. They are also likely to be sifting through a large pile of proposals at the time they come to hold your submission in their hand. Therefore, you need to do everything possible to be personal and memorable, and get your hard work read. This means thinking about the way you present a proposal, including the language you use to convey it, the look and shape of the document (whether physical or electronic), and how it gets from your desk (or screen) to the 'yes' pile at the funder's board meeting.

With this in mind, when preparing to submit your ask, you should consider the following:

- the extras to submit with a proposal;
- how to write and finesse all the relevant documents to make them powerful and persuasive;
- getting it all in front of the right person at the right time and then following up in an effective way.

Case study: the Make-Believe Charitable Trust[1]

Let's imagine a fictional grant-maker called the Make-Believe Charitable Trust. It gives away grants of £5,000 to £100,000 to a broad range of general charitable purposes. A board of five trustees is chaired by Sir Gordon Make-Believe, the grandson of the original founder, and is supported by a small staff made up of a grants administrator and his secretary.

The administrator, Mr Blake, receives around 80 proposal submissions in any given week – almost 20 times the number of grant awards the trust could possibly fund. Mr Blake works hard to assess every single proposal to determine how it fits in with the trust's charitable objectives, although in reality this is an almost impossible task given the volume and breadth of the submissions. It is 10am and already he has received 12 emails and has 17 pieces of mail in the post to sift through, from charities as diverse as the Fobbington History Museum, Books for Children International, the Hedgehog Rescue Association and the Hemmingsville Hospice Society.

Mr Blake is just about to open the next letter packet when the phone rings. It is Sir Gordon, who says, 'Listen here, I've heard about a fantastic project that I think we need to look at. There should be something on your desk about it.'

Mr Blake leafs through his current pile. 'Is it Books for Children or the Fobbington History Museum?'

'No, no, no. It's about hedgehogs getting caught in bonfires. Dreadful stuff. Put it on the shortlist, will you? Jolly important we protect those creatures; terrible state of affairs for the ecosystem and something needs to be done about it.'

This submission has clearly used a strategic approach.

The auxiliaries

When Mr Blake opens the envelopes on his desk, there will be more than proposals to look through. Even in an online application form, there will be supplementary elements that need to be considered with just as much care and attention, including cover letters or emails and any additional appendices.

Cover letters

Reportedly, one third of recruiters know whether they will hire someone within the first 90 seconds of an interview.[2] A cover letter is like that initial minute and a half, because it is the very first thing someone will read. Based on the content and style of the document, your reader is likely to have formed an idea in their mind about whether they are interested before they even turn to the first page of your main proposal.

A cover letter need not necessarily take the form of a traditional paper letter. It may be an email and, in the case of many grant-makers' online application systems, it may be an additional communication rather than a requirement. If you have built a good relationship with the funder, writing to your key contact to inform them of your submission is courteous and will also help to keep you front of mind. Whatever form it takes – this chapter will call it a cover letter for simplicity's sake – the purpose of this piece of the submission is to fully introduce your proposal and ignite the interest of the recipient. This may be a trustee or decision-maker, or a gatekeeper such as an administrator, with the power to put your proposal in front of the trustees – or to discard it before it even sees the light of day.

A great cover letter will:

- **Be addressed to a specific person:** avoid 'Dear Sir/Madam' and ideally address it to someone you have already spoken with, who is expecting the submission.
- **Summarise the proposal:** provide an overview of the problem, your solution, your need and the specific request you are making to the funder (how much, what for and over how many years).
- **Get the reader's attention:** explicitly link your project with the funder's (relevant) priorities and point out the mutual fit. Make clear that this is not a circular mailing but that you have thought carefully about how the funder can achieve its own objectives through your work.
- **Be clear and concise:** preferably use no more than one side of A4 (two at most) but cover the salient points. You don't need to include all the evidence cited in your proposal (since you are introducing the proposal, not replicating it); rather, this should be a brief yet compelling argument for your funding need.
- **Avoid generalisations:** for example, unless requested, it's usually best not to send any general brochures, which could appear impersonal or look like a blanket appeal.
- **Be bold and assertive:** use confident language that doesn't take the onus away from the funder. Accidentally apologetic phrases such as 'if you might have the time to consider, or know of anyone else who might be able to help' reduce the assuredness of your request.
- **Be well presented:** use a plain font and a letterhead that looks professional, has *up-to-date* information on it (such as current trustees, patrons and so on) and doesn't take up half of the page. For emails, include a professional e-signature with appropriate contact details.
- **Reference any key funder information:** especially do this if you don't expand upon it in your main proposal. You might mention any proposed benefits of the funder's support if it is a company (such as publicity) or any funding already received from other sources. Citing the support of others helps to endorse your cause and reassures the funder of your credibility.

- **Include personal contact details:** this is so that the grant-maker can actually get back to you. Include your or someone else's specific contact information rather than a general enquiries email address or phone number.

- **Sign off with brevity:** avoid long-winded pleasantries at the end (for example, 'We do hope you will be able to give favourable consideration to our request for support at this time and if you would like to discuss the initiative further, or require any further information, please do not hesitate to contact me at xxx or by telephone on xxx'). Your contact details will hopefully already be at the top of the letter, so instead a short 'Thank you for your kind consideration' may do the job better.

- **Be signed by someone else:** where possible, the cover letter is best signed by someone either known to or known by a key individual at the funder. This influential person is endorsing the proposal and the work presented within it, which in turn increases the likelihood of it being considered seriously.

This last point refers back to the idea that other people, not just you as the fundraiser, will ideally play a role in your approach (see page 63). Of course, sometimes the person signing the cover letter *will* be the fundraiser. If you have developed a strong relationship with the recipient, it makes sense for the cover letter to come from you. If you are wearing many hats, such as being the project manager as well as the fundraiser, or perhaps even the leader of your entire organisation, you yourself may be the strongest and most appropriate signatory. Most of the time, however, it will be somebody else. It may be a peer connection, which is particularly fitting if they introduced you to the funder at the beginning of the relationship. Alternatively, it may be a senior member of staff, such as a programme director or CEO. Whoever it is, it is important that they are respected by and relevant to the funder. Choosing a signatory with a bit of clout also shows that you really care about the funder's support, having made the effort to enlist a significant other.

> Cover letters are often more important than people think. They are the first introduction to your project and your organisation and therefore must be carefully thought about. Sometimes we take what seems too long on cover letters, but they can be what makes the trust or foundation actually look at your application. We carefully consider sign-off for each application, whether it be a personal or professional connection or a senior title which will enable our approach to get through the gatekeeper and to the right person.
>
> Kate Billingham Wilson, Head of Partnerships and Philanthropy, ABF The Soldiers' Charity

Appendices

Along with the cover letter, in whichever form, there are often other documents that are submitted in support of a proposal. Your appendices might include:

- **literature**, such as annual reports, a copy of your accounts or relevant organisational publications;
- **additional project information**, such as planning documents or extra budgetary detail;
- **longer case studies**, if they are highly pertinent to the proposal but too lengthy to include within it;
- **visual material**, such as architectural drawings for buildings or photographs of complex equipment.

The stress here is on the word 'might', as you should avoid sending anything that could be deemed as unnecessary or a potential waste of printing and postage costs. Some grant-makers will love receiving your annual report, but others will put it straight in the recycling bin if they simply don't have the capacity to look at it. Others again may delight in reading through your organisational business plan, while others might find it an excessive use of paper. Similarly, recent accounts are a common requirement but grant-makers can and often will find them online rather than needing you to send a copy. The best thing is to just ask before including any extra bumpf, particularly for postal submissions.

> I always remember the words of the director of one large trust. When asked about sending additional information along with a proposal, he used to say, 'Please don't send hernia-inducing packages.' This has been a helpful thought when I've been applying for funding directly or working with a client organisation that wanted to include all kinds of supporting materials. I also translate this message to current times and consider if the file size of a document and any attachments is the equivalent of 'hernia-inducing', especially since many email systems have a block on large file size emails or they go straight to the 'junk' folder.
>
> Gill Jolly, Director, Achieve Consultants Ltd

The other thing to be wary of is relying on appendices for core proposal information. A grants secretary once told me that seeing the words 'see attached' results in an instant rise in their blood pressure, as they simply do not have the time to be cross-referencing between documents. For capital projects, this might be unavoidable – for example, it may be impossible to work building plans into the body of a proposal. That's absolutely fine and funders will understand this, as long as it is necessary and relevant.

Standing out from the pile

With so many proposals to leaf through, how do decision-makers choose which are the best? Even the most fantastic project in the world still needs to be presented in a way that is engaging and compelling. It is important, therefore, to consider carefully *how* your proposal is written, to persuade the reader to support your cause.

Writing persuasively

The goal of all fundraising materials (proposals, letters, notes and so on) is to convince the reader that your work is worth investing in. Your aim is to write in a way that is:

- **engaging:** catching the reader's attention and holding their interest;
- **enthusing:** inspiring them with your own passion and conviction;
- **encouraging:** moving them enough to want to act.

Persuasive writing needn't involve lengthy descriptions and elaborate language. In fact, you will often be working to tight spaces or word count restrictions, so you will need to find ways of writing persuasively while also maximising the effective use of space.

Two helpful techniques are implementing the three Ts and avoiding the three Vs.

The three Ts

Have you ever fiddled about with the margins of a Microsoft Word document, trying to fit as much as possible onto a page without it looking crammed? We've probably all done it. However, rather than attempting to squash in more text, it is better to make fewer words work harder. The three Ts are excellent ways to do this and are best adopted from the outset, but can also be used to edit pre-written text. The three Ts are:

- **Tone: use an upbeat, positive and enthusiastic manner.** You want to sound confident that what you are talking about is both powerful *and* achievable, while also balancing this with an undertone of urgency and importance that compels the reader to feel that something really must be done about the issue at hand. Conversely, you want to avoid any tone that could be portrayed as whingy, complacent, apologetic or even hectoring. Tone should also be consistent throughout. Be particularly wary if you are cutting and pasting information from other sources; make sure it reads as if the final result was written by one person. It should also reflect the style of the recipient – for example, a formal tone or a conversational tone, depending on the type of funder.

• **Tenor: use the active voice rather than the passive voice.** Make sure your subject is the one performing the action and not having it done to them. 'Annie was helped by our programme staff to...' is written in the passive voice; it is harder to read than 'We helped Annie to...', which is in the active voice. The active voice sounds more dynamic and, as an added bonus, usually uses fewer words. For instance, 'We work closely with...' communicates the same information as 'A partnership has been established between our organisation and...' but reads much more easily and effectively, particularly if someone short on time is scanning your document. Practise writing in the active voice to get into the habit of using it, and see whether you can spot the difference when reading other texts.

• **Tenacity: use confident and affirmative language.** The words we use can portray different senses to the reader, even if two versions literally mean the same thing. For example, 'We will...' sounds bolder and more assured than 'This projects aims to...', which is more wishy-washy. Similarly, 'We expect to...' is stronger than 'We hope that...'. Part of tenacious language is using wording that focuses on users' needs over your own – for example, 'We will overcome isolation by bringing older people together twice a week' is more powerful than 'We need a minibus once a fortnight.' Likewise, 'essential costs of services' is a phrase that is more engaging and sounds more steadfast than the phrase 'overheads and management costs' or 'administrative and promotional costs', even though they all describe the same thing.

The three Vs

While adopting the three Ts, we also want to avoid particular danger zones – or the three cardinal sins of persuasive writing:[3]

• **Verbicide: distorting words so that they no longer make sense to the reader.** This includes using jargon, specialist words and unexplained acronyms that only you or those in your field would understand. We can take this completely for granted when we are used to hearing particular phrases within our organisation that have become standard internal language (such as 'a learning organisation'... what is that, a school?). Some jargon phrases are especially popular in the charity sector and can almost become second nature but may irritate or confuse a reader: 'local agenda', 'lived experience' and 'soft ask' are all common culprits that may be clear to us but baffling to someone else. Caution should similarly be used with unexplained acronyms, which may not be obvious to the reader; for example, 'ACF' could be used when referring to the Army Cadet Force, the Australian Conservation Foundation or the Association of Charitable Foundations.

• **'Verbitis': inflaming words to the point where they pretty much lose all meaning.** While you will need to clearly describe the context and the importance of the issue, it is easy to fall into the trap of using words that are a bit clichéd. Superlative words and phrases such as 'unique', 'urgent', 'desperate plight' and 'major new initiative' are best avoided as they have become so overused in funding proposals. Stick to facts and figures to emphasise needs rather than dressing them up with those kinds of words. Your reader is likely to find themselves in their own desperate plight if they read about any more urgent and unique major new initiatives!

• **Verbosity: waffling on too much or using more words than necessary.** It's easy to get into unnecessary detail, which uses up space as well as being irrelevant. Take out any redundant information, for instance 'We are a registered charity…', which is likely to be obvious already from your letterhead (and probably only worth mentioning if you are *not* a registered charity). Also be wary of being over-wordy. Sentences with too many words, clauses, hyphens or brackets can be quite difficult and confusing to read – especially when something could be expressed much more succinctly (such as through tightened language and shorter sentences, which could do the same job and relay a similar meaning) – otherwise by the time the reader has actually reached the end of the sentence, they will probably have forgotten what on earth you were trying to say. Or, don't use twelve words if three will do. For instance, 'From the evidence that has been collected, it can be concluded that…' versus 'Research shows that…'. This is easier to read, as well as saving that precious word space.

Say what?[4]

Here are some real-life examples of the deadly three Vs. What do these phrases mean?

1. Grain-consuming animal units.
2. Localised capacity deficiencies.
3. High-quality learning environments are a necessary pre-condition for facilitation and enhancement of the ongoing learning process.
4. If there are any points on which you require explanation or further particulars, we shall be glad to furnish such additional details as may be required by telephone.

5. It is important that you shall read the notes, advice and information detailed opposite then complete the form overleaf (all sections) prior to its immediate return to the council by way of the envelope provided.

Answers:

1. Farm animals such as cows, pigs or sheep.
2. Traffic bottlenecks.
3. Children need good schools.
4. Please ring if you have any questions.
5. Please read the notes opposite before you fill in the form. Then send it back to us as soon as possible in the envelope provided.

Knowing your audience

The preceding examples show how complicated language is unhelpful and can be off-putting to readers. With that being said, you also need to use the appropriate level of complexity for a given funder. Many grant-makers – particularly larger and institutional funders – are experts in their field, and in these cases it is suitable to use terminology and a level of detail suitable to the recipient's expertise. Conversely, when writing for someone with little knowledge of the subject area, do ensure your language is not so simplistic that you could come across as patronising. Your funder research (see chapter 3) will play a key role in informing what level of technicality you should use. If the funder has publications or a website, have a good look at the kind of phraseology they use. It is also worth noting down any terms or buzzwords used in any of the funder's talks or seminars, if you are able to attend or watch them. Even better, if you have successfully engaged with the funder interpersonally, you should have a strong understanding of the grant-maker's level of knowledge and perception of the problem being discussed.

Your writing style will also have to be adapted for different types of grant-maker. Corporate foundations may respond best to terms and phrases that reflect their business goals. A small family charitable trust may be drawn to more emotional language. A large statutory funder may require an emphasis on outcome-based language in order to fulfil its assessment criteria. The aim is to speak the grant-maker's language, rather than imposing your own. This is one of the reasons why blanket mailings and pre-prepared documents, where the funder's name is inserted into a mail merge, are not such a great idea.

House style

Many organisations have a house style, which may include written documents using a particular font, colours, and even specific words and phrases that fit with the overall organisational brand. The challenge is to incorporate this alongside the style of the grant-maker, by tailoring your language and the level of detail you provide as outlined above.

Ideally, you will want to mirror the discourse of the funder, much the same way as you would in a verbal conversation. You're aiming to create synergy and enable the reader to feel that you are both on the same page, and therefore more likely share the same ideals and goals. Meanwhile, you do also want to display your own organisational identity, so the funder can get to see and know you. There is a balance to find between these two potentially competing aims.

It is certainly worth having an internal discussion about brand identity and how this might need to be portrayed in external communications to fit in with the rest of your organisation. Particularly for larger charities, which may have a marketing team that sets the rules, it is helpful to discuss where there could be flexibility in funder materials and where specific words, images, logos, colours, fonts and so on must be used.

Proofreading power

Even if you are on a super-tight deadline – actually, *especially* if you are on a super-tight deadline – be sure to prioritise proofreading. Research shows that only around half (54%) of grant-seekers have someone else review fresh proposals and that 39% only proofread for the very largest bids.[5] This simple step is so important, for proposals of any size, and should be factored into the submission timeline so that there is adequate opportunity to make any changes. Our brains are designed to fill in the gaps when reading,[6] so you could read the same sentence five times yourself and still miss a mistake. At least one person should proofread a proposal (and any accompanying cover letter or other written materials you plan to submit), and more than one person for particularly significant or dense proposals.

Proofreaders are worth their weight in gold, as they look at everything with a fresh perspective, just like the recipient. For this reason, it is ideal if the proofreader is someone with little or no knowledge of the project. Volunteers can be very handy for this. Not only might they pick up on typos (which are quite irritating to a funder with a huge pile of proposals to read) but they can also see whether everything makes sense to a lay person, check it flows well from one section to another, and assess how compelling the proposal is to someone learning about the issue for the first time.

Ask your proofreader to look out for:

- spelling and grammatical errors (especially the spelling of any names and addresses – including in letter headings);
- repetitive words and phrases;
- assumptions (including any assuming phrases such as 'We all know that…', because we surely don't all know!);
- assertions that are not backed up with evidence, such as research or statistics;
- rhythm and flow (sections should be well ordered and lead on to each other in a way that makes sense);
- inconsistencies in tone and style;
- numerical errors (including budgets or figures – these need to add up correctly).

There are some fantastic courses and workshops available on writing skills; these are well worth exploring to look into all these areas in greater detail. These resources need not be specific to proposal-writing – courses on storytelling and writing to influence are equally relevant to grants fundraising materials.

> The applications that really stand out are the ones that are brought to life through stories and examples. We want to understand how charities support their beneficiaries, and the best way to do this is through stories from the people they have helped. Specifically, we want to see the depth of that support and the journey they have taken people on, highlighting the impact of their work and difference it's made to someone's life. As much as we want to see how charities use a person-centred approach in their work, we understand that a charity can't meet all the complex and unique needs of the people who come for help. When this is the case, we want to understand how charities work with other organisations to plug the gaps so that their beneficiaries can receive holistic support.
>
> Harriet Stranks, Director of Grants, Lloyds Bank Foundation

The strategic submission

Once you've crafted all your documents and given them a bit of finesse, it's time for the big submission. A strategic approach, like the one Sir Gordon received (see case study on page 107), is about much more than simply popping something into a post box or clicking 'send'. It will have involved thought and planning on the part of the fundraiser, considering what and who else may be of influence at this critical stage. This is where other elements come into the picture, including recommendations from peers, distinctive little details to make the proposal stand out, and the strength of your existing relationship with the funder. Indeed, it is the human factor that can make all the difference to an already-excellent proposal and really make it shine more than the rest.

The personal touch

In a world of computers and typed correspondence, little personal touches can make a lot of difference even for formal grant-makers. This is the kind of detail that shows thought, and it can give you the edge among the other submissions.

Your funder research (see chapter 3) will help you to get an idea of what is appropriate, and not everything will be suitable for every funder. However, simple, effective personal touches could include:

- a courtesy call to inform the grant-maker that your submission has gone out and to check it's been received or to see whether any further information is needed (remember that phone calls are very effective and greatly underused – see page 76);
- a suggested follow-up, such as a site visit or relevant invitation to learn more about the project;
- a cover slip accompanying your letter, proposal or other documents, with a handwritten personal note;
- a handwritten envelope – particularly for a private or family foundation, or where the person opening the post is likely to be a decision-maker or someone influential to the decision-makers;
- a handwritten sign-off rather than a photocopied signature;
- an additional note, where proposals have had to be submitted online and have little opportunity for a personal touch.

Large, popular charities probably need to pay the most attention to these areas. They may be fighting the perception that they are big, impersonal corporate machines that already receive plenty of funding from elsewhere. This is where the personal touch can really help – if our fountain-pen-loving trustee at the start of this chapter is anything to go by, the little details can indeed be quite significant.

Right place, right time

Back in chapter 4, we looked at the issue of timing (see page 65) – choosing the best point in the relationship to submit the proposal to maximise your chance of success. In the ideal scenario, you will have established a good rapport with the funder and have enlisted the support of any helpful endorsers or peer connections, and the funder will already have gained a strong understanding of the issue and need at hand through your pre-proposal engagement. Having achieved all these things will place you in the strongest position to submit your proposal, and it is always worth waiting until this point rather than jumping in to submit something at the first opportunity.

This is especially important for organisations that deal with emergency funding, such as those that work with natural disasters or projects where unforeseen incidents require immediate funding. Where the groundwork has already been laid, securing emergency funding is that much easier. Where the preparatory work hasn't been done, it is very difficult to get funding at short notice, however desperate the need.

Some grant-makers have rolling application deadlines, meaning that you can submit your proposal whenever you like and it will be considered at the next board meeting. This is helpful if you want to have more relationship-building time and submit the proposal at the optimal time. However, note that if the next meeting is in May, the funder is likely to need proposals in at least a month before that, so it is worth calling to check before you plan your submission timeline. If there is a specified deadline, make sure you have everything ready in good time beforehand – many fundraisers have experienced the beads of sweat when they find themselves right down to the wire when putting in a proposal. Plan in advance. The printer could, and probably will, run out of toner. If the online submission deadline is 5pm, assume there will be an office-wide IT-related disaster at 4.58pm. Plus, be sure to factor in time for that crucial proofreading (see page 116).

Sometimes a submission will happen in person, on the spot. This may be in a meeting context, where the proposal is formally presented to a funding decision-maker, or as part of a round of formal presentations, as is popular with numerous institutional funders. It can be intimidating making a funding request face to face, but it is helpful to remember the power balance explored in chapter 5 (see page 77): you are asking for a *partnership* and funders need charities to fulfil their objectives in the same way that charities need funders to fulfil theirs.

The follow-up

Let's go back to our busy grants administrator, Mr Blake (see case study on page 107). As we've explored, he has hopefully opened his post to find an engaging cover letter from someone at the Hedgehog Rescue Association whom he knows and respects. This letter, the proposal itself and other accompanying documents have been carefully crafted, personalised and submitted in good time for the specified application deadline.

Meanwhile, the Hedgehog Rescue Association has developed a two-pronged approach plan. As well as developing a relationship with Mr Blake, the charity has engaged a peer to connect with the main decision-maker, Sir Gordon Make-Believe. At the key point of submission, the charity has worked with this individual to send an endorsing follow-up communication to Sir Gordon.

There may not always be an opportunity to take this peer-to-peer approach. But it is always worth having a good think about what or who could come into play to supplement and boost your submission at this stage. Note that this is not about going around or behind the back of a gatekeeper (see page 75). Rather, it is about nurturing a genuine, meaningful and influential relationship, or using an existing one, which can be a very effective strategy.

Dear Gordon,

It was wonderful to see you at the club last week. As discussed, I'd be grateful if you could consider the Hedgehog Rescue Association (HRA) at the next meeting of your trust. The work they are doing to prevent hedgehogs meeting the most horrendous fate, which in turn has a destructive impact on the natural habitat, is most impressive. As you know, I am personally involved and am passionate about these important animals, which do so much for our countryside and are deserving of our protection. I hope you don't mind that I've asked Penny at the HRA to put something in.

Warmest thanks and I look forward to our next round of golf.

Yours ever,
Roger

The stage is set.

Spotlight: when it's a no

Unfortunately, your efforts won't always result in a grant. Even the best fundraisers will have plenty of unsuccessful approaches, and facing rejection is just a less fun part of the job. Many grant-makers will notify you of the outcome either way, and others will ask you to assume you have been unsuccessful unless you hear otherwise. It is disappointing to learn you haven't secured funding, especially if it has taken months or even years to develop an approach. However, receiving a rejection is rarely, if ever, the end of the line.

Rejection can often be used as an opportunity to build further rapport. It provides the chance to pick up the phone, to glean guidance about what could've been done better, and to review your proposal and approach plan. Only 55% of grant-seekers ask for feedback from funders (and 26% only ask for it on their largest bids),[7] which is missing a trick since many grant-makers are willing to provide it – some quite extensively – and just finding out why you were unsuccessful is enormously helpful.

The Institute for Voluntary Action Research (IVAR) facilitated discussions for 27 foundations as part of its Community of Practice for open and trusting grant-makers. IVAR noted that receiving feedback on unsuccessful proposals is a critical part of achieving more open dialogue between charities and funders.[8] The institute reported that from funders' perspective, there was always a reason for the choices they made, and they felt that sharing these reasons is important in developing a respectful relationship. Funders further noted that feedback is helpful for them too, as it helps them to keep the quality and effectiveness of their decision-making under close scrutiny.

In addition to giving helpful feedback, there may be other ways a funder could support you following a rejection. Perhaps a key trustee could become an adviser, matching their expertise to an area of your work. Someone with a good network of contacts can be invaluable – possibly even resulting in more funding for you than a direct grant would have done – and may have useful connections in other areas, such as with corporates or major donors. It is also worth asking funders whether they have any suggestions about who else you might approach for support and whether they would be willing to make an introduction if so.

For larger proposals, it can be very useful to undertake an internal review process after the submission. Sport-for-development charity Sported find this a valuable way of gleaning important lessons from the application process:

> After we submitted a particularly complex bid to an institutional funder, we ran an internal 'wash-up' session for everyone

involved. This meant finding an external facilitator to run the session – someone who knew the organisation and who the team felt comfortable with, but who was not involved with the bid. They helped the group to set some ground rules and enabled everyone to have their say, focusing on what went well and what could be improved next time. The critical thing was to do this before we found out whether the bid was successful or not. This meant that the discussion wasn't influenced by the outcome. We were not distracted by the temptation to pat ourselves on the back or by the need to understand why the bid hadn't been successful, but focused on the process of developing the application. We had a very constructive session, which has informed how we put subsequent bids together and strengthened internal support for fundraising.

Sam Dixon, Trusts and Statutory Fundraising Manager, Sported

Finally, keep a good record of the feedback and conversation, even if it was a no. It could be very helpful for the next time.

Conclusion

A proposal submission can be much more strategic than simply filling in a form online or putting something in the post. Done well, the submission stage can use your previous research and engagement work to find funder-appropriate ways of cutting through the piles of other requests.

In a nutshell...

- Consider what extra documents need to be carefully crafted alongside your proposal, and what little details or additional endorsements might have a positive influence.
- Even the best projects need to be presented in a persuasive way. Use writing techniques, such as implementing the three Ts and avoiding the three Vs, to maximise the power of your words within a limited space.
- Always have at least one person proofread your proposal before it goes out to check for errors, logic and flow, and how it comes across to someone seeing it for the first time.
- Make your submission as personal as you can – where possible, rely on the power of an endorsement or peer-to-peer connection to strengthen your approach and use a follow-up communication as an extra cultivation opportunity.
- Rejection is rarely the end of the line. A 'no' is really a 'not yet', and there is always the opportunity to take feedback, re-engage and re-evaluate your approach for future funding success.

Notes

1 Adapted from Tim Finn, 'Making First Contact', in *Trust Fundraising*, edited by Anthony Clay, London, Directory of Social Change, 2011, pp. 57–8.

2 'How interviewers know when to hire you in 90 seconds' [web page], Undercover Recruiter, 2020, https://theundercoverrecruiter.com/infographic-how-interviewers-know-when-hire-you-90-seconds, accessed 7 December 2021.

3 Based on Mike Eastwood and Michael Norton, *Writing Better Fundraising Applications*, London, Directory of Social Change, 2010, p. 73.

4 Based on examples supplied by the Plain English Campaign for Mike Eastwood and Michael Norton, *Writing Better Fundraising Applications*, London, Directory of Social Change, 2010, pp. 72–3.

5 *Funding Social Change: How can grant-seekers and grant-makers collaborate to better serve our communities?* [PDF], KEDA Consulting, 2021, www.kedaconsulting.co.uk/wp-content/uploads/2021/06/keda_consulting_funding_social_change_a4_50pp_V2.pdf, p. 23, accessed 7 December 2021.

6 Natalie Wolchover, 'Breaking the Code: Why yuor barin can raed tihs' [web article], Live Science, www.livescience.com/18392-reading-jumbled-words.html, 9 February 2012.

7 *Funding Social Change: How can grant-seekers and grant-makers collaborate to better serve our communities?* [PDF], KEDA Consulting, 2021, www.kedaconsulting.co.uk/wp-content/uploads/2021/06/keda_consulting_funding_social_change_a4_50pp_V2.pdf, p. 23, accessed 7 December 2021.

8 Liz Firth, Eliza Buckley and Keeva Rooney, *Towards More Transparent Application and Assessment Processes: Practical ideas from open and trusting grantmakers* [PDF], Institute for Voluntary Action Research, 2021, www.ivar.org.uk/publication/towards-more-transparent-application-and-assessment-processes, accessed 7 December 2021.

CHAPTER EIGHT

Thanking, managing and stewarding your funders

Introduction

We have come to the last part of our journey through the approach cycle, or the top layer of the sponge cake model (see figure 1.2). While thanking, managing and stewarding your funder are placed at the end of the cycle, they are certainly not the final destination. It is better to think of these elements as setting the stage for the next approach to your funder, taking you back around the cycle from the best possible position. This stage is therefore one of the most important in grants fundraising, and yet it is also perhaps the most undervalued.

This is probably because this stage comes *after* the receipt of a grant. Since achieving the funding seems like the main goal, thanking, managing and stewardship can often end up being a bit of an afterthought. This stage is also one of those areas that is commonly talked about but less often acted upon. A great many grants fundraising strategies will feature the need for excellent funder care to maintain and grow future partnerships. However, in reality, it often gets demoted down the priority list as a bit of an optional extra – something you do if and when you get around to it (which is never, because there are too many other pressures from trying to get new funders in and all those proposals out of the door).

With that in mind, let's have a look at why the stage of thanking, grant management and stewardship is so important:

- It concludes a positive grant-making experience for the funder.
- It is respectfully consistent – it doesn't leave the funder feeling like you have lost interest now you have what you want.
- It leads to repeated and increased long-term funding and partnerships.
- These in turn will enhance your good reputation, which attracts more new prospects and leads to greater funding.
- Not that many of us are doing the best possible job in this area. One survey found that 38% of grants fundraisers did not do *any* kind of additional stewardship with their funders.[1] So if you deliver amazing funder care, you will stand out.

Happily ever after

Since we're talking about relationships here, we'll use the analogy of a marriage. Perhaps one person spots the other across a crowded room, asks their friend about them, learns they have a lot in common and decides that this could be the one they've been looking for. They go over and introduce themselves, and the two get on brilliantly. After various dinner dates, they decide to get hitched. The wedding is stunning, and the couple are clearly well suited to each other. They have a fantastic honeymoon in the Maldives and post pictures of themselves snorkelling together on Instagram.

And then they come home. They practically stop speaking to each other, live entirely separate lives, file for divorce after a month and both start looking for a new spouse.

What went wrong?

Sometimes we can be guilty of allowing our relationships with our funders to fall apart in this way. It's not intentional, but we damage funding relationships when we simply forget to prioritise our current funders because we're so busy chasing new prospects. It can also be disappointing for funders if we have put lots of time and energy into engaging with them, but then appear to drop off the radar once we have the money in the bank and no longer feel the need to court them. As the list in the chapter introduction highlighted, this is not such a great strategy. Prospecting is important, but it should never be at the expense of your existing funder relationships. Consumer marketing research shows that the probability of selling to an existing customer is 60% to 70%, whereas the probability of selling to a new prospect is 5% to 20%. Existing customers are also 50% more likely to try new products and spend 31% more compared to new customers.[2] While these are commercial market figures, the same principle applies to fundraising: in terms of income generation and growth, your current funders are *the most* fruitful area to focus on.

Thanking, management and stewardship: what's the difference?

Thanking, grant management and stewardship all have the same end goal: they aim to make funders glad of their decision to support you. Thanking does this by making a funder feel valued and appreciated. Good grant management does it by demonstrating that you are making a difference with the grant. Stewardship does it by involving and inspiring the funder as an engaged partner in your work. All of these in turn increase the likelihood of a repeat or uplifted (i.e. larger) grant, and encourage other funders to come on board.

Thanking and stewardship are often confused, since there is some overlap between their intentions. Using our sponge cake model (see figure 1.2 on page 14), where funder care is the whole top layer, it can be helpful to think of the stewardship element as the proverbial icing on the cake.

Stewardship goes beyond the essentials of good thanking and reporting – it involves thinking both creatively and strategically about how to bring funders closer to your organisation and mission, of which they are now an integral part.

The cake topping is often noted as 'optional' on a recipe. Many charities have found, however, that focusing on stewardship in addition to good thanking and grant management can reap quite extraordinary rewards.

> During my time leading the individual giving team at an international development charity, as part of our stewardship strategy, we tested the concept of noticing when a donor gave an increased donation. We selected a test group and acknowledged their increased gift with a hand-written card. The copy wasn't rocket science; the message was very simple: 'Thank you for your particularly generous gift.' We tracked donor behaviour over the next 12 months, and at the end of the year, 23% of donors who received the card doubled their donations in the following year, compared to 16% of those who did not receive the card. The test group also gave 174% more compared to 116% in the control group, and the test resulted in a return on investment (ROI) of 155 to 1 in just 12 months.
>
> This approach can be easily applied to grant-makers, and there is no need to stop at increased support – recognising repeat donations, marking the anniversary of support or just sending a simple random appreciation message that is not attached to (but might be nicely timed just ahead of) an ask can yield impressive results.
>
> Rachel Hunnybun, Director and
> Fundraising Consultant, Blakely Inc.

Since all three elements of this top layer are important, let's explore them in turn.

Thanking funders

Good thanking is timely and expected. It may take the form of a phone call, an email, a letter or a combination of these things, and it should gratefully acknowledge the grant and confirm any reporting requirements and timelines. Some grant-makers also require grantees to complete a formal receipt or an official form; if needed, you should send this with your thank-you letter. This is all ideally done within a day or two of receiving the grant or offer letter. Interestingly, only a third (34%) of grant-seekers say they respond to the funder within a day, and nearly a fifth (17%) take longer than three days, while another 2% never thank at all.[3] As a general rule, the sooner you thank the funder, the better.

Great thanking, in turn, is not just timely but also strategic and personal. It will involve – at the appropriate levels – anyone else who played a part in your approach, such as connectors, senior staff, relevant programme staff and possibly even beneficiaries. For example, you might make a personal thank-you call to the grants administrator yourself, arrange a call from your CEO to the funder's CEO, and organise for a handwritten note to be sent from one of your trustees to the chair of the funder's board. The thanking process will also link back to your planning stage (see chapter 4), as it will consider what type and level of acknowledgement will be most appropriate for and valued by that particular funder. For example, your acknowledgement may involve using social media channels to publicise and celebrate the grant if that is a medium used and appreciated by the grant-maker. Or, if appropriate to the size of the grant, it might include listing the funder's name in a public place, such as on a plaque or within a published report.

The personal touch comes into its own with thanking. Think about when you've received a thank you for something yourself. A round-robin letter with your name added after the 'Dear' will have made you feel a lot less appreciated than a handwritten card, thanking you specifically for your gift and describing what it meant to the recipient. The round-robin letter will probably have been pleasant to receive and you may have scanned it quickly before putting it in the recycling bin. The handwritten message, however, is more likely to have made you feel good and glad that you gave the gift, and you might even prop it up on a shelf as a happy little reminder. This is what great thanking is all about. Personalised notes, cards, calls and emails all serve to ignite the part of grant-making that is enjoyable and satisfying, whether for the staff of a formal institutional funder or for a family pursuing their philanthropic endeavours through a charitable trust.

Things to consider to ensure great thanking include:

- Remembering people who played a part in achieving the grant whom you need to thank personally – the grants administrator, the trustees, the grants director?

- Thinking about whom each of these people would most like to hear from – you, your CEO, a beneficiary, the chair of your board?

- Talking about the funder more than yourself – use the word 'you' more than 'we', as the focus should be on the funder's experience of grant-making.

- Using the power of the handwritten note – in the digital era, the effort and warmth of personal snail mail are often highly valued and will stand out against other thank yous received.

- Considering what types of acknowledgement would be appreciated by that particular funder (in addition to any conditions of the grant) – the grant-maker's name listed on your website or annual report, or highlighted as a case study in a publication?

Generally, the larger the grant, the more you will want to think in detail about these questions. Personal thanking, by its very nature, should be less standardised across your funders, and one of the challenges with this can be parity. If you are fortunate to receive a lot of grants, you cannot feature all of the grant-makers in your annual report. Furthermore, you won't want someone to notice you waxing lyrical about a particular grant on Twitter and wonder why you haven't posted anything at all about their own organisation's grant, or to feel less valued because they weren't invited to your annual gala dinner whereas other funders were.

Setting out a written policy is very helpful in this area, as it provides a systematic approach to thanking funders in different ways according to the level of their grant. The following section looks at this in more detail.

Creating an acknowledgement policy

A funder acknowledgement policy (also known as a recognition policy) aims to provide structure to the thanking and recognition of funders across different giving levels. Discretion and flexibility are required, since different funders will have different wishes and requirements. Some funders will have no desire for acknowledgement on social media, for example, whereas others may actually require it as a condition of the grant. However, an agreed policy is a useful guide for justifying – internally and externally – your thanking activity and for inspiring ideas about new ways to recognise your funders' contributions. It might look something like table 8.1.

TABLE 8.1 Example of a tiered acknowledgement policy

Grant level	Thanking activity
Small (£0–£5,000)	• Thank-you call to be made by fundraiser within 24 hours of receipt of grant or notice of grant (email if no phone number available) • Reporting requirements to be confirmed during the call and noted (on database or other recording system) for future action • Official thank-you letter to be issued within 48 hours of grant receipt, restating agreed reporting requirements • Any influencers to be informed and additional thank-you calls, emails or notes to be arranged as appropriate • All calls, emails, letters, receipts, and handwritten notes and cards to be saved or scanned onto database or other recording system • Grant letters to be scanned onto database or other recording system and original hard copy filed for auditing purposes

Medium (£5,000–£25,000)	All of the above, plus: • Offer to acknowledge in published annual report • Call and additional written communication (handwritten note, letter or email) to be sent from programme manager to funder's grants staff or equivalent role
Large (£25,000–£50,000)	All of the above, plus: • Offer to publish acknowledgement on social media channels • Offer to meet CEO or invite to high-level event • Call and additional written communication (handwritten note, letter or email) to be sent from CEO to funder's CEO (or equivalent)
Major (£50,000–£100,000)	All of the above, plus: • Offer to publish acknowledgement on website • Offer to attend personal meeting with chair or invite to exclusive event • Call and additional written communication (handwritten note, letter or email) to be sent from board (or chair) to funder's chair (or equivalent)
Exceptional (£100,000 and above)	All of the above, plus: • Offer of bespoke naming opportunity • Offer to attend personal meeting or other exclusive opportunity (e.g. private event) with ambassador • Call and additional written communication (handwritten note, letter or email) from president or ambassador via appropriate channels

These are examples, so think about the different acknowledgement options or exclusive opportunities your organisation might be able to offer to significant funders. The tiers can be tailored entirely to your grants income levels and number of funders. If you tend to receive fewer and smaller grants, it is still helpful to have at least four levels of distinction – perhaps 'small', 'medium', 'large' and 'exceptional' with financial levels attributed as appropriate. It is always worth having the 'exceptional' level, as you should regularly ask yourself the question, 'What would we do if someone gave us £1 million?' (or whatever a truly exceptional or transformational grant would be for you). This question will make you consider your internal capacity to receive, spend and manage such a grant, and what an exceptional level of thanking could look like for your organisation.

It is helpful to have your acknowledgement policy written up, included in any induction packs for new fundraising team members, and regularly read and reviewed by the grants fundraisers in your organisation to ensure everyone is thanking funders consistently and working to an officially agreed standard. It is also important to share the document with other fundraising departments, if your organisation has them, to ensure consistency and that all teams are aligned on their thanking and recognition activity.

Some grant-makers wish to remain anonymous. In this case, you may need to ascertain just how anonymous they require to be and potentially even make their identity known only to a small number of relevant internal staff. While anonymous funders will not desire the publicity of social media, inclusion in documents or naming opportunities and the like, there will still be private, personal and bespoke ways of making them feel thanked and valued.

Grant management

The goal of grant management is to demonstrate that you are using the funds well and achieving what you set out to achieve. Some funders will have specific reporting forms whereas others will simply ask for a progress report, in a format of your own choosing, usually six or twelve months after you receive the grant. Whichever the reporting format, it is important to be totally and completely honest with your funder. Absolutely share and celebrate the successes of the project, but also talk about the challenges and even failures if there are any. Funders want to see this honesty, as well as the lessons learned and ways in which your organisation has adapted around difficulties. Reporting this information will increase your credibility and give the grant-maker better insight into the issue at hand.

> We don't just want to hear about your successes. We want to know when things don't work out; why they don't go well; and how you learn from them and use that knowledge to move forward. We are always really impressed when an organisation can talk about things that have gone wrong and what it has done to change as a result as easily as it can talk about its successes.
>
> Hannah Lim, Funding Manager, Esmée Fairbairn Foundation

Questions to ask yourself during your grant reporting include:

- What have you achieved against the SMART outcomes (as outlined on page 94) set out in your original proposal?
- What do you have left to achieve?

- What have been the main challenges?
- What monitoring and evaluation targets or milestones do you need to report on?
- How is the work promoting best practice, both in your organisation and more widely?
- Is there a demonstrable social return on investment (known as SROI) you can talk about?[4]
- Do you have any case studies from the reporting period that can bring your work to life?
- Can you include the voice of a beneficiary within your reporting?
- Do you have any relevant and recent photographs, videos or other engaging material of the work to date?
- Have there been any noteworthy internal changes (such as key project staff, your CEO or your chair) that the funder may wish to know about? If so, ensure you pass this information on immediately, rather than the funder reading about it in the sector news.
- Have any external events, such as economic or political developments, had any effect on your project or other funding relevant to it? For example, government policies around statutory funding opportunities may change and have implications for your project or wider organisation if you are reliant on such funding sources.
- Has anything at the funder changed? Have there been any staff, influencer or decision-maker changes where new relationships need to be established, or new policies that may put a different focus on your funded work?

If there have been changes affecting your organisation, or there are proposed changes afoot, consider whether the funder could be involved in any consultations as a key stakeholder. This will be especially relevant to larger grants or funders, or those that have a high cumulative value to your organisation that may have valuable advice and expertise to share. Taking them into your organisation's confidence on internal issues, where appropriate, also shows that you value their input and opinion. This is all part of bringing funders into the fold, as they become less of an external party and more of a partner and, ideally, a long-term part of your charity's family.

One of the keys to strong grant management is cultivating good internal relationships. Your programme and project teams, fundraisers, and any other key staff involved in the project or funder relationship will all come into play over the life of the grant. As the fundraiser, you will be the one to liaise with and co-ordinate all of these dynamics, so that progress is reported back to the funder effectively and with the level of detail required. Creating a project team for large grants, with these different internal stakeholders, can be very helpful.

For larger or more complicated projects, it can be valuable to sit down with the project team and map out a timeline for the grant and any associated activities. This can include any reports that are required (to enable programme staff to factor in the time needed to provide the information), potential events and project visits that could enrich the funder's understanding of the work, and any general organisational activities that could serve as additional points of contact. Table 8.2 provides an example of a timeline.

TABLE 8.2 Sample project grant timeline

Feb	Mar	Apr	May	Jun	Jul	Aug	Sep	Oct	Nov	Dec	Jan
Grant received and funder thanked Project begins		Invite funder to project visit	Project visit		Six-month progress report due		Send copy of annual report	Invite funder to event	Event Invite funder to carols concert	Send holiday card Meet staff at carols concert	Twelve-month progress report due

These contact moments, such as invitations and meetings that are additional to the grant requirements, are an important way of valuing a funder beyond formal reporting. Research shows that 87% of grant-seekers say they always report back to funders on time, but only 66% communicate with funders outside the formal application or reporting window, and almost a quarter (24%) do not invite funders to project visits or events.[5] You will be missing opportunities if you only do the bare minimum. Good grant management will go beyond the essentials of reporting and treat the funder as a partner in the work, engaging them in the project as it progresses.

> Once, when reviewing the income streams at a medium-sized national charity, I saw the team were successful at securing trust support but not brilliant at getting repeat gifts. Further digging revealed that the finance director undertook all trust reporting and only included a spreadsheet of the finances to show how money had been spent in terms of the budget. She felt this was the role of finance and as a result there was no ongoing relationship with the funder. The trust team then took over the reporting and account management, supported by both finance for the figures and services for cases studies and impact information. After adopting this 'team approach', the picture soon changed.
>
> Gill Jolly, Director, Achieve Consultants Ltd

Do also remember to note any and all communications, reports, invitations and project visits in your database or using another method of record-keeping. Setting up alerts, even as basic as calendar reminders, can also help you to keep on top of reporting deadlines and the time needed to gather information in advance.

Just as with the proposal and accompanying documents, grant reporting should be as bespoke to the funder as possible. It is also well worth re-enlisting your proofreader (see page 116) before you send off any reports. Once again, consider whether any additional oomph could accompany your communication, such as a personal note from a beneficiary or senior or programme staff.

When things don't go to plan

Occasionally, you will have to report back to funders with less positive updates. Perhaps the project has stalled or has had to change completely since the point of your original proposal. Or perhaps you have received more funding than expected for a particular project and now you need to return some or all of the grant – a nice problem to have, but one that leaves you in a bit of a sticky spot with the funder.

In situations where you need to break difficult news to a funder, the best course of action is transparency. Grant-makers know that projects and charities can encounter challenges along the way and that plans sometimes need to change. If you can tie these changes in to the monitoring and evaluation systems you have in place, then all the better, as you will be demonstrating the effectiveness of learning as you go and adapting to changing needs, which is the point of all good evaluation. Where you have overspent or underspent a grant budget, again, it is honesty that is required both contractually and ethically. You may also be surprised at how understanding a funder may be in allowing you to redirect funds to a different project or need.

Creative stewardship

We looked earlier at how thanking, management and stewardship are different, with stewardship being the creative and strategic element of bringing a funder closer to your organisation. The creative part of this involves using big-picture thinking to come up with inspiring ways of connecting with a funder and its motivations for giving. The strategic part is about being intentional and considered in how you carry out your stewardship, including deciding who you want to inspire and how.

It is helpful to include the word 'creative' as a reminder that this is all about being original (doing something that nobody else is likely to have done) and inspirational (aiming to enthuse and ignite a passion for your work within your funders). It is about embedding your funders into your organisation and aiming to take your relationships to the next level, beyond the transactional and into true partnerships. Stewardship of this sort takes resources, but most of this will be time and effort rather than money. Stewardship activities themselves need not be costly and in fact it is often the cheaper ideas that are the most effective, such as a simple personalised note or a handmade card from a child beneficiary. Funders usually do not want charitable funds to be spent on glitzy items or expensive plaques, and the power of thoughtful and measured stewardship is not to be underestimated.

> Many funders like us operate with small teams across large geographic areas, so we can't get out to visit our grantees as much as we would like. Therefore, feedback, stories and engagement with our grantees is very valuable and appreciated. Some of the feedback we have received has been really heartening. We have had grantees send us video tours of a new building that we helped fund. This was great, as we could share this with our own donors too.
>
> Stories and case studies are always so impactful, as they can bring together real examples of change from a human perspective. We use our social media as a platform to share both what's going on in our community and also the extent of our work.
>
> We know we are only one funder in the 'ecosystem' of a grantee's funding world, but even a simple email telling us about the impact of the grant can demonstrate just how much it means to them as an organisation and also to the individuals that have benefitted from it. This is a process of engagement that we try to maintain throughout the life of a grant, encouraging grantees to share their feedback with us rather than making it a part of any formal reporting. We find this much more useful and have now started to review our overall end-of-grant reporting process.
>
> Caroline Taylor, Chief Executive, Essex Community Foundation

One of the leading UK fundraising departments at NSPCC identified stewardship as being so critically important to the charity's income that a dedicated team was set up to focus on it. The Stewardship and Engagement Team supports fundraisers across the trusts, major donors and corporate departments, delivering high-value supporter experiences such as events, visits and meetings with senior and front-line staff.

> Stewardship is at the heart of our fundraising at the NSPCC and we work hard to keep our supporters engaged and committed to the services we provide for children. Around 90% of our funders are those who gave the year before and our income from trusts has doubled over

> the past four years. This is due to our focus on a high level of stewardship, which involves maximising giving and personal engagement through creative means and fostering funders' commitment to our work.
>
> Edgar Sutcliffe, Head of Major Giving, NSPCC

While most charities are unlikely to have the resources to dedicate a whole team to stewardship, even those with limited capacity for fundraising should have funder stewardship high on their list of priorities. Some organisations have found it helpful to hold regular stewardship inspiration meetings, where the team or group of colleagues gather around to think of creative ways to steward a particular funder. The premise here is to ask the question, 'If the sky were the limit, what would we do to make this funder feel close to and inspired by our work?' Creative ideas should flow from there. Another way to think of this is that you are aiming to create extra-special moments for your funders, to wow them.

Wow moments

Rob Woods, founder and director of Bright Spot, coined the phrase 'wow moments' for fundraising, inspired by the book *The Power of Moments* by Chip and Dan Heath.[6] Woods describes a 'wow moment' as a critical strategic moment designed to make someone *feel* something rather than only evaluate a piece of information intellectually.[7]

You can apply this mindset to help you with various fundraising objectives, not just for stewardship and thanking, including motivating funders to want to meet you or attend an event (for instance, by creating a personalised video message) or making your events and meetings more inspiring (for instance, by planning a 'reveal' moment or using props to bring a story to life). In stewardship, wow moments are a powerful way of engaging funders with the work they have supported and go far beyond the information they might receive in a formal report. The aim is to create a unique experience, in addition to what they might already know factually, which makes you and your organisation more memorable.

This is especially effective with significant grants, where the impact or reach that the funding has enabled can be difficult to convey on an emotional level. For example, 'You have helped us to reach 1,500 children in need' might sound like an impressive statement. But visually representing those 1,500 children in some way is a more powerful way of demonstrating the extent of the impact. Alternatively, you might focus on the story of just one beneficiary out of that 1,500, or the particular activity your work has undertaken, to bring the impact to life on a meaningful level.

What might this look like in practice? As stewardship moments like this are unique and funder-specific, there are no set rules about creating them. But below are some real-life examples of charities that have developed intentional wow moments for their grant-makers.

- We made a picture with over a thousand fingerprints on, to represent all of the young people the trust's funding had enabled us to reach. It was visually effective and moving to see the impact of the support displayed in that way. The grant-maker loved it.
- As an international development charity, it's difficult for us to convey the impact of our work overseas, so we have used virtual reality goggles – loaned to us by a corporate supporter – to show funders interactive videos of the impact of our work in the field. We have had some very formal grant-makers in tears when they've seen the videos.
- For our largest ever funder, we sent in a framed painting by one of our child beneficiaries. It cost us about £10, for the frame. It hangs on the funder's office wall to this day.

All of these ideas were inexpensive but extremely effective as they used a creative way of demonstrating impact to the funder. It was also unlikely that the funders had experienced anything like this before – the ideas were different, emotional, inspirational and memorable, but still very relevant to the funded work.

Moments like this do not have to be grand gestures. Small and more regular stewardship activities, such as sending an e-update, a holiday card or an event invitation, can be done in a highly personalised and powerful way with some thought and creativity to make them more impactful for the recipient. What simple things might enable funders to experience your organisation's work on another level, to 'wow' them?

Storytelling

Another important tool in your stewardship toolbox is storytelling. Storytelling is the art of bringing a funder closer to your work through real-life examples. Stories are powerful, as they demonstrate your impact on a relatable level.

Meaningful stories could come from:

- **Beneficiaries:** if your services benefit people, sharing a personal story of how the project has brought a positive change in their lives can be very effective, especially if it is told in their own words.
- **Project or programme staff:** particularly consider those who have a fiery passion for their work. Staff can have inspiring first-hand experiences that show a unique perspective to the funder.

• **Volunteers:** accounts by volunteers are less common, but these people often have powerful stories behind the giving of their time and may be personally affected by either the issue or the work your charity does to address it. They will also be close to your organisation, and possibly the project, while providing a slightly external, objective perspective.

• **Fundraisers:** perhaps the most underused storytelling is our own. Fundraisers can provide an interesting viewpoint, since they are usually exposed to the need, the project and the inner workings of the organisation. Think about your own experiences and motivations – what inspires you about working where you do, and why do you do it? Particularly where a good relationship has been built with individuals at a grant-maker, communicating your own experiences and associated emotions can be very impactful.

This final point raises the issue of fundraisers being exposed enough to the work to garner their own personal stories. It is an important investment for fundraisers to have the time and opportunity to see the work they are raising money for, not only to better understand it but also to develop their own experiences that can be relayed to funders. This also helps with the engaging and enthusing part of persuasive writing for both proposals and reports, as explored in chapter 7 (see page 112).

A grants fundraiser for the hospital charity The RUH Charitable Fund found that taking time to gather stories, both of her own experience and that of colleagues and patients, had a powerful effect on her funder reporting:

> Rather than simply emailing a ward sister or member of staff asking whether they had any stories they'd be willing to share, I ventured into the hospital we support and asked to start shadowing staff members. Not only was this an eye-opening experience but also staff felt appreciative that I was finding out about their role in the hospital while meeting more patients and hearing about their struggles first hand. One of my first shadowing experiences led me to the cancer support team, where I heard how they themselves had been impacted and was told about things that their patients often found especially hard. I was able to share my experience with trusts and foundations that receive our quarterly progress report, which focuses on our campaign to fund a new cancer centre. For the first time, funders replied and they sent cheques! There was no ask or expectation, but changing the style of the report – from bullet points on the progress of the build to hearing what was happening in the here and now – shifted the dynamic and opened up conversations with our funders. Getting to know staff and patients reignited my passion for fundraising and gave me the confidence to introduce the human element into my reports – and in turn build better relationships with our funders.
>
> Rosie Scott, Partnerships Officer, The RUH Charitable Fund

Stewardship stories can be gathered and told in all sorts of ways. Written, audio, video and other communicative forms are all powerful ways of sharing stories, and gathering a range of these case study materials is a worthwhile task (just be sure to get permission to use them). It is also worth thinking about what stories could be helpful for funders to promote within their own reports, websites or social media, or to share with their board of trustees as examples of their grant-making impact.

Milestone mapping

A milestone is a significant point in a funder's cumulative giving to your organisation. It is a fantastic opportunity for stewardship, as it is a special moment in your relationship to acknowledge and celebrate. For lower-level grants, a noteworthy milestone may be £50,000 or £100,000 if the funder has given to your organisation over several years or a decade. For large grants, it may be a very high figure, such as £1 million over time. Use your own judgement about which milestones should be noted and celebrated for a given funder. Many grant-makers will not even be aware themselves that they have given so much cumulatively, making it all the more special that you have noticed and acknowledged it. Other types of milestone you might choose to monitor and celebrate could be the number of years a funder has been supporting your cause, or the number of beneficiaries their specific funding has enabled you to reach.

Creative stewardship can really flourish with milestone celebrations, as you can tailor your plans to the funder's interests and style as well as incorporating the particular number identified. Visual representations are often very effective, such as in the 'wow moments' examples (see page 136). Or you might choose a specially arranged visit to a project, a personalised photobook, or a video message recorded by a prominent person such as a patron or ambassador. These are not just suitable for individual major donors – they are very much appropriate for grant-makers of all kinds.

Once again, whatever you produce need not be costly; the point is that you have noticed, thought about the milestone, and done something special to mark the moment and express your gratitude in a meaningful way. Much like receiving an unexpected gift from a friend with a 'saw this and thought of you' note, it is the sentiment that hits home.

Some databases will have a function that automatically generates a funder's cumulative giving figure, but with others you may need to keep a manual record to keep track of noteworthy milestones that are approaching. Be careful to double-check your records too, to ensure that you are acknowledging the correct milestone and are not missing any critical funding history information within your files.

Spotlight: the power of 'thank you'

In 2018, the Institute for Sustainable Philanthropy published a report on thanking.[8] The researchers interviewed 15 experts in acknowledgement communications and conducted tests to gather evidence documenting the benefits of thanking funders. Among the results of this fascinating and comprehensive report, the findings included:

- Where donors had given an average of three gifts, sending them a thank-you letter about the difference their gifts had made increased the average value of future gifts by 60%.[9]
- Where donors had given many (an average of 16) gifts, sending a thank-you letter affirming the special relationship the funder had with the organisation's CEO increased the response rate of a follow-up renewal letter by 10%. The same effect was found with thank-you letters to this group that affirmed the donor as being a wonderful person.[10]
- Thanking donors for the difference they made to a single beneficiary was more effective than thanking donors for the difference they made to thousands of beneficiaries.[11]
- Organisations that had an effective thank-you programme in place also had fundraisers that felt better about their job – thanking can inspire fundraisers as well as funders.[12]

The overarching finding of the report was that great thanking is an incredibly powerful tool in increasing funder retention and lifetime value (i.e. cumulative giving to your organisation). The researchers also estimated that if thank-you communications to funders are done in a consistent and engaging manner, organisations have the potential to increase the 'good feeling' of their donor base – and therefore their ongoing support – by a minimum of 20% over five years.[13]

Indeed, many charities have found that a focus on thanking and stewardship pays real dividends. The major national health charities Sue Ryder and Macmillan Cancer Support both prioritise this area of their grants fundraising within their team strategies:

> As a team we have a key performance indicator (KPI) around getting positive supporter feedback. We plan supporter journeys for trusts around key communication moments throughout the year. This approach helped us secure £425,000 in three grants from a grant-making foundation over two years, the first two being capital grants and the third, an unrestricted grant of £250,000, coming from the foundation's COVID-19 response

fund. Alongside our reporting commitments, our chief executive met the funder's CEO and our team met with the funder's grants manager to understand the foundation's priorities and perspectives on the relationship. We also made a personal thank-you video from staff at our charity's new centre that the foundation had funded, tagging its CEO on social media and offering a virtual tour of the new centre. The CEO responded to our thank-you video with this message: 'This is a very thoughtful and lovely video. Thank you. We are glad to be involved and don't feel as though we deserve the thanks... you are doing the great work!'

Andy Watts, former Head of Trusts, Sue Ryder

For us at Macmillan it's all about balance – driving new business while also giving the space needed to nurture and grow existing support. Exceptional stewardship is central to that. That means really getting to know donors and their motivations, involving them meaningfully in the work they're supporting, and always looking to grow and deepen the relationship. That's the only way you can move from a transactional ask-based portfolio to one built on long-term, strategic relationships with funders – viewing them as partners in realising the change that, together, we want to see in cancer care.

Francis Webster, Foundation Partnerships Lead,
Macmillan Cancer Support

Conclusion

Rather than thinking of thanking, grant management and stewardship as the endpoint of a funder–grantee relationship, it is better to think of it as the cyclical link to continuing a fruitful partnership. Focusing efforts on this area sets the stage to go around the approach cycle again, from a place of strength, leading to larger and repeat grants.

In a nutshell...

- Thanking is an essential, expected part of the grant journey and should involve other key individuals to be the most impactful. An acknowledgement policy is a helpful way of ensuring funders are thanked in a systematic way.

- Good grant management involves working closely with project staff to produce timely reporting but hinges most of all on honesty and transparency. Funders want to hear about your challenges as well as your successes.

- Stewardship is a strategic part of funder management. Its aim is to bring funders closer to your cause, cement the partnership and even help you to reap great rewards in the form of future grants.

- Great stewardship involves creativity: developing thoughtful, bespoke 'wow moments' for your funders that inspire and ignite a greater passion for your work.

- Putting focused attention, energy and resources into thanking, management and stewardship is one of the most effective strategies for achieving significant income growth from grant-makers.

Notes

1 *Funding Social Change: How can grant-seekers and grant-makers collaborate to better serve our communities?* [PDF], KEDA Consulting, 2021, www.kedaconsulting.co.uk/wp-content/uploads/2021/06/keda_consulting_funding_social_change_a4_50pp_V2.pdf, p. 30, accessed 7 December 2021.

2 Khalid Saleh, 'Customer acquisitions vs. retention costs: Statistics and trends' [web article], Invesp, www.invespcro.com/blog/customer-acquisition-retention, 11 November 2019.

3 *Funding Social Change: How can grant-seekers and grant-makers collaborate to better serve our communities?* [PDF], KEDA Consulting, 2021, www.kedaconsulting.co.uk/wp-content/uploads/2021/06/keda_consulting_funding_social_change_a4_50pp_V2.pdf, p. 29, accessed 7 December 2021.

4 See the NCVO website for more information about SROI at https://knowhow.ncvo.org.uk/studyzone/measuring-your-social-return-on-investment-how-to-get-started

5 *Funding Social Change: How can grant-seekers and grant-makers collaborate to better serve our communities?* [PDF], KEDA Consulting, 2021, www.kedaconsulting.co.uk/wp-content/uploads/2021/06/keda_consulting_funding_social_change_a4_50pp_V2.pdf, pp. 30–1, accessed 7 December 2021.

6 Chip Heath and Dan Heath, *The Power of Moments*, London, Bentham Press, 2017.

7 See 'Breaking the script – three ways to inspire your supporters' [blog post], Bright Spot, 2018, www.brightspotfundraising.co.uk/breaking-the-script-three-ways-to-inspire-your-supporters, accessed 5 April 2022.

8 Jen Shang, Adrian Sargeant, Kathryn Carpenter and Harriet Day, *Learning to Say Thank You: The role of donor acknowledgements* [PDF], Institute for Sustainable Philanthropy, 2018, https://static1.squarespace.com/static/5e99b731e7ec45190a6bc6a6/t/5ec59003a6524a5dc5eeff44/1590005764382/Learning-to-Say-Thank-You_eBook-27122019.pdf, accessed 7 December 2021.

9 *Ibid.*, p. 5.

10 *Ibid.*

11 *Ibid.*, p. 36.

12 *Ibid.*, p. 13.

13 *Ibid.*, p. 5.

CHAPTER NINE

Troubleshooting

Introduction

As we have seen throughout our exploration of the approach cycle (see figure 1.1), all grant-makers and therefore all approaches and proposals are different. However, they follow the same footprints of relationship development as we get to know, engage and nurture a mutually beneficial partnership. Along the way, it is also common to come across bumps in the road while navigating the most effective path on the grant-seeking journey.

Following a call put out on social media, over 50 fundraisers from grant-seeking organisations kindly submitted their questions for this final chapter. Between them, they raised some of the more common and challenging issues that can arise in this form of fundraising. This chapter addresses a selection of the most frequently recurring themes, which broadly fall into four categories:

- managing internal structural and ownership issues;
- navigating income targets and expectations;
- handling funder relationship complications;
- getting around grant-seeking limitations.

Managing internal structural and ownership issues

'Who should "own" the funder relationship?'

Imagine a charity with three high-value fundraising departments: a corporate fundraising team that looks after company partnerships, a major donor team that looks after relationships with high-net-worth individuals, and a trusts fundraising team that looks after charitable trusts and foundations. Then we have Ms Givealot, who has made her personal fortune through building up her FTSE 100 company. The company has its own foundation, which derives its income from the dividends of the company's profit and is managed by company staff. Ms Givealot is well connected and knows many philanthropists, and she also sits on the boards of two significant charitable trusts herself. Which team should manage this relationship?

Grant-makers can often cross over various fundraising departments, given the nature of the individuals involved with funders' decision-making and the different origins of their money. As well as there being a natural crossover with corporate and major donor fundraising, there can also be a crossover with legacies (such as when a trust is left in someone's will), direct marketing (such as where a trustee is also an individual giver), and community fundraising (such as when someone at the grant-maker takes part in an event).

Even when there are numerous multi-departmental touchpoints, it is usually helpful for one person to be the primary relationship manager for any given grant-maker. This is to ensure that there is someone aware of, recording and co-ordinating all planning and communication to avoid any disjointed or inappropriate approaches. Imagine the chaos, for example, if Ms Givealot were to receive three propositions from different parts of the same charity. Where there is no obvious answer to who this main relationship manager should be (a family foundation, for example, could easily be argued to sit under the remit of either a trusts or a major donor team), one option is to have a joint approach where different teams work together to achieve a joint target or split any income received across the two internal budgets. Alternatively, you might create a soft, informal target or key performance indicator (or KPI) around cross-team working, which can be a motivating way to reward internal collaboration outside direct income generation. In any case, you will need to have a person or people who oversee the activities of everyone involved.

The key is co-ordination. While different teams may be vying to achieve their own income targets, the overarching priority is the relationship between the grant-maker and your organisation as a whole, and working together to make the approach that will be best for your beneficiaries. If the personnel in the charity in the example above can work together well, they can use the expertise across all three teams to make the most appropriate approach and potentially maximise support across all three areas of Ms Givealot's giving potential, by engaging her in a co-ordinated and strategic way.

'How should we structure our grants fundraising?'

An issue that flows from ownership is how an organisation ought to structure its grant-seeking function. Should a trusts team include statutory and institutional fundraising? Does grants fundraising fall under major gifts, alongside major donors, or should it be a separate team? And should regional offices have local trusts within their remit or should all grant-makers fall under a national head office?

There is no single answer to this kind of issue, as many fundraisers will tell you after having undergone various restructures, sometimes merging and then unmerging departments multiple times over the course of a decade.

> I once worked in a department which covered major donors, trusts and institutions together, then separated trusts and major donors into different teams, then added statutory funders into trusts, then had a larger restructure to merge more broadly with the corporate department. All within the space of five years!
>
> **Trust fundraiser**

The advantage to having more specialist teams is that it promotes particular expertise within those areas. The disadvantage is that it can create internal competition, where teams are focusing on their own income budgets and may be less likely to work together on areas of funder crossover.

The right structure for your organisation is therefore the one that promotes the best collaboration. Whether you have one large department or several distinct teams, useful resources such as case study materials, project information, proposals and feedback should all be shared to avoid duplication and to promote good internal working. Funding approaches must also be well planned and communicated internally, ideally with any connections regularly discussed and noted in some form. A good central database will help to capture such links and to ensure that no approaches are made that encroach on someone else's related plans.

> It's important that your internal structures work for your organisation and your supporters. It is helpful to have agreed roles and responsibilities and terms of reference for working with different teams, as this can clarify the desired goals for collaboration. We have also developed a scoring checklist where we score funders on a set of criteria – such as how they are set up and where their funding is derived from – to determine which team should manage them. For example, this might help us to determine where a particular corporate foundation would best be managed. Leadership is also very important for collaboration as your leaders set the tone and culture of how much cross-working occurs between different teams. This needs to go hand in hand with the agreed roles and responsibilities and terms of reference. An ultra-high-net-worth individual could be both a trustee of a grant-maker and a CEO of a FTSE 100 company, so it's in a charity's interest to collaborate internally rather than have different teams working in silos.
>
> Ryan Wilkinson, Head of Foundation Partnerships, UNICEF UK

Remember also that while a grant-maker might sit within your department, it may be someone else who is best placed to be the frontperson in the relationship. As we explored in chapter 4 (see page 63), grant-seekers are often the ones behind the scenes conducting the show; it might be front-line staff or regional colleagues who are most appropriate to be the face of your organisation.

'How can I work effectively with programme colleagues on grant-maker approaches without losing control of the overall relationship?'

Grant-makers often like to speak directly to programme staff rather than fundraisers. In particular, funders with their own technical expertise may prefer to liaise with like-minded experts and have detailed discussions about the work on a programmatic level.

This can be very helpful, as long as programme staff are aware that you, the fundraiser, need to be privy to any conversations between them and the funder and involved in any follow-up actions. One way to go about this is to ensure that programme staff see the value of your involvement. As the co-ordinator of the approach and the developer of the proposal, you are the one who has overall oversight of the relationship and can take notes, record meetings and draft follow-up communications. If you can make this clear at the outset, working together with your programme colleagues can be a really positive and fruitful experience for all involved.

Unfortunately, it is not always easy to control who makes contact with your potential and even existing funders. Many fundraisers have had to have difficult conversations with colleagues who have taken matters into their own hands and perhaps been unaware that there was a carefully planned approach in the works from their fundraising colleagues.

Some charities find it helpful to communicate an internal standard operating procedure (often referred to as an SOP) to ensure that all departments of the organisation understand the importance of going through fundraising colleagues when liaising with grant-makers. This is a formal route to take and will need to be undertaken with tact and care. For most charities, though, a less formal conversation will usually suffice to simply explain the value of being joined up and working together to maximise connections and thus income for your cause.

> We arranged a meeting with a large charitable foundation where, as the conversation got going, the director we were meeting with began to look quite confused. It transpired that he had already met with some of our programme colleagues in the field on a recent overseas visit, who had presented a completely different proposal to what we were discussing with him. It was obvious that we'd had no idea about it, and it looked like we had different priorities to our other colleagues. We came across as disjointed and it undermined my role as the relationship manager, as my colleagues had gone directly to the funder without seeing the need to involve me. We needed to have an internal conversation to explain that any funders, even those heavily involved with programming on the ground, must have centrally co-ordinated communications to avoid such mishaps in future.
>
> **Grants fundraiser**

Navigating income targets and expectations

'How do I manage internal expectations around grants income?'

Managing income expectations is a common challenge for grant-seekers. Senior staff, board members and programme colleagues in particular may understandably want to know exactly how much is going to be raised and by when. This can create significant internal pressure for fundraisers, as expectations may differ from what is realistic.

Internal colleagues can be surprised to learn that grants fundraising, by its nature, is not a quick win. It takes time to find, research, engage and cultivate grant-makers, as explored throughout the earlier chapters of this book. An average approach might take anywhere from 6 to 18 months, or longer for a particularly large or complex funder.

The speed and success of a grants fundraising programme will also depend on your organisational readiness for this form of income generation. Chapter 4 explored the necessary ingredients for this readiness, including the information-gathering, evidence of need, credibility and reputation-building work required (see page 56). For organisations new to fundraising, it will take time and resources to gather all of these things, and senior leadership may need to understand that grant-seeking is unlikely to be successful without this investment.

Another common misunderstanding is that grants fundraising is about quantity: churning out as many applications as possible with the aim of achieving a return of 10:1 (ten applications required for every successful grant) or some similar blanket success rate. There certainly is a scientific element to projecting grants income, based on the amounts you are applying for and how often. However, it is helpful to explain to senior leadership that good grants fundraising is about quality over quantity, and the art of finding connections, developing persuasive proposals and building relationships is much more effective than sending out mailings en masse. With this in mind, it is useful to monitor the number and value of applications that you send out, but it is less useful to conceive of this as a target to gauge how well you are doing. You could send out 100 proposals asking for £50,000 each but be more successful with fewer, carefully crafted approaches.

Engaging your wider colleagues in the process is a great way of showing them how grants fundraising works in practice. Chapter 2 looked at the peer review and qualification process (see page 31), in which you can involve senior staff, trustees and programme colleagues, both to help with prospecting and to provide insight into the techniques and time frames required. A presentation at a board meeting can also be very helpful for trustees, both to help them understand what grants fundraising entails and to engage them in supporting your efforts through their own networks. Where there continue to be challenges with internal expectations from senior staff, it may be worth enlisting the support of a grants fundraising consultant to provide an external, objective perspective on what it is realistic to achieve for your organisation.

Finally, it is important to celebrate wins and to include the rest of your organisation in doing so. Some teams ring a bell when a grant is received. Some send an email to the whole organisation to share good funding news. Whatever you do, include any relevant programme staff and board members who would benefit from hearing about your successes and learning more about your grant-seeking activities.

'What is the best way to set grants fundraising targets?'

There are many different methods used to set grants income targets, but the most common is to allocate a percentage likelihood against the amount you are asking for from each funder. A simple spreadsheet can capture this (and some databases will be able to generate a report of this information for you), with funders listed in the first column and your projected income plotted across 12 months' worth of rows, as shown in table 9.1.

TABLE 9.1 Sample income forecast spreadsheet

	Jan	Feb	Mar	Apr	May	Jun	Jul	Aug	Sep	Oct	Nov	Dec	TOTAL
Funder 1	£5,000						£5,000						
Likelihood	50%						50%						
Risk adjusted	£2,500						£2,500						**£5,000**
Funder 2				£20,000									
Likelihood				25%									
Risk adjusted				£5,000									**£5,000**
Funder 3										£10,000			
Likelihood										100%			
Risk adjusted										£10,000			**£10,000**
TOTAL	**£2,500**			**£5,000**			**£2,500**			**£10,000**			**£20,000**

As the sample table shows, the amounts that you have asked (or plan to ask) for are plotted in the appropriate rows according to when a grant would be most likely to be received, based on any known decision-making meetings or grants disbursement dates. Since we can assume that not all proposals will be successful, a likelihood percentage is then applied to these figures, which results in an adjusted projected income total.

Likelihood percentages are subjective. Some charities choose to apply high-, medium- and low-risk percentages, based on their previous success rates, such as 70% for a low-risk proposal (where there is a strong relationship or good indication of the funding being received), 40% for a medium-risk proposal (where there is a relationship and reasonable fit but less strong indication of success), and 10% for a high-risk proposal (where there is little established relationship). Others may use a sliding scale to input likelihood percentages, such as 100% for committed funds down to 5% for cold approaches that are less likely to succeed. The more years you have been projecting your income, the more accurate you will become at it, as you will get a better idea of what is realistic for your organisation. It is important to note, however, that no income projection method will be perfect and certainly none can forecast the occurrence of external factors, such as economic turbulence, which may affect grants income. This is simply a system for organising your approaches and giving a best-guess estimate based on the information available.

Understanding your own return on investment (ROI) in grants fundraising is extremely valuable for more accurate income projection. In a survey of 248 UK-based grant-seeking charities, most organisations admitted to not knowing what their current ROI was and that it was not something they regularly measured. In the same report, grant-makers responded to this finding by saying that they were both surprised and disappointed that so many charities are unaware of their success rates.[1]

Whichever income projection system you use, the main thing is that it should be a bottom-up exercise, rather than top-down. This means that you should be looking at your funders and range of prospects first, making projections based on those individual approaches and totalling everything up, rather than plucking a figure from the air and trying to fiddle the figures to make up the sum total. This can sometimes be challenging to explain to senior leadership, but it is an important point to stress if there are grants income expectations that are less than realistic.

Finally, the same survey mentioned above had a particularly interesting finding – that 94% of grants fundraisers do not feel that they are maximising their grants income potential.[2] This is a fascinating figure, as it might suggest that the vast majority of grants fundraisers feel pressured to increase how much they can raise from this particular source, despite the fact that grant-making disbursement levels have remained fairly consistent over recent years.[3] The question remains whether as a sector we are setting unrealistic income growth targets from a finite income source.

'How do we prevent over-reliance on a small number of funders?'

This is an important question, as grant-seeking charities will often have one or more major funders upon which they largely depend. Large grants are wonderful, but you do need to be careful about putting all your eggs into one basket and becoming over-reliant on too few funding sources. This becomes a problem if a sudden change occurs, such as a funder having a dramatic drop in its income or changing its criteria, or unforeseeable external economic factors coming into play.

Ensuring there is a wide-enough spread in your funder base is the best protection against over-reliance. You can spot potential over-reliance by looking at your forecast spreadsheet (see table 9.1) and noticing any major grants that would skew your overall income up or down depending on whether they are successful. If you are managing a lot of funders, you can also divide them into categories (according to grant size) to get a sense of whether any single category is too heavily or too lightly represented. Having a mix of funder sizes – small, medium and large – is a good strategy, and drawing up a simple pyramid such as that shown in figure 9.1 is a helpful way of seeing whether you are over-reliant on any one category.

FIGURE 9.1 Basic funding pyramid

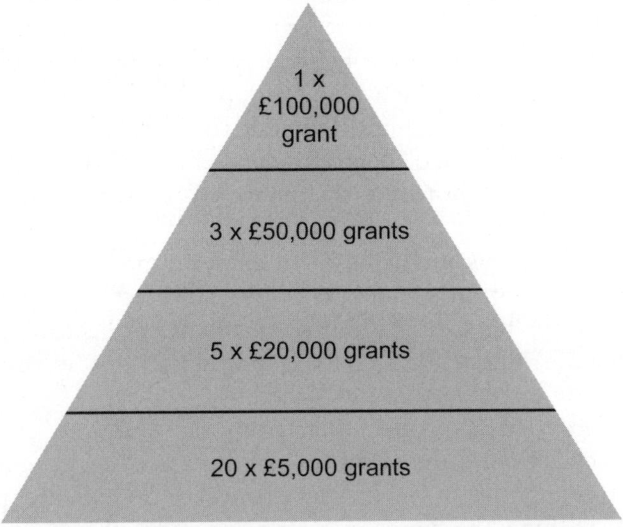

In this simple example, there is a spread of income projected across all categories, meaning that while the loss of the largest grant would be significant, there is still substantial income projected from other sources. Where this exercise reveals that income is heavily skewed towards the top of the pyramid, it is important to review those relationships regularly and ask the question of how you would mitigate a potential loss of funding from that level. Measures might include long-term planning to continue high-level funding after a particular grant runs out, or diversifying your income across other funders and funding types.

If you do have particularly large grants, it is especially important to ask the question of what will happen – and what the internal expectations will be – when a particular grant finally runs out. Is the anticipation that you would find another big grant to fill the gap? Or is it accepted that your income will simply be lower in subsequent years? It is also worth thinking well in advance about how to nurture major grant-maker relationships so that you already have the next proposal in mind, rather than waiting until a grant has run out and starting back at the beginning to try and secure another large grant.

It is worth noting that funders, too, may be interested in your funding mix and may have queries or concerns about whether your organisation relies on one or only a few income sources. Being able to explain your fundraising plan will be an important part of demonstrating how you will mitigate such risks.

Handling funder relationship complications

'Should we avoid being funder-led?'

We looked earlier at how researching funders, to both identify and understand them, should come before the proposal-writing stage (see chapters 2 and 3). This is because having a general proposal that you then try to fit around a funder can look like a blanket appeal and is unlikely to result in success. However, it is very important not to misunderstand this as being the same as being funder-led. Being funder-led means developing a project or programme itself – not just the proposal – around the interests or desires of a funder.

An example of this might be if an exciting grant opportunity comes up and your organisation decides to create a project to fit the criteria, in order to achieve the particular funding. While the project might be aligned with your organisational aims, if it is not what you were going to do anyway, then you have become funder-led.

Being funder-led is problematic, from the perspectives of both the grant-seeking charity and the grant-maker. You need to have already identified your funding needs, including proposed or existing projects and plans, before seeking the funds necessary to carry them out. Otherwise, your work is being dictated by something other than the need and you can easily lose focus and alignment with your original vision and mission. Most grant-makers also do not want this scenario. Funders want to see that you have identified and evidenced your need, and that your project forms the basis of the best solution to the problem. Grant-makers do not wish to see charities redesigning their activities around funding opportunities for the sake of securing funding rather than the best outcome for their beneficiaries.

> While there may be some criteria from funders which you may consider adopting – for example, we like to work with charities that are themselves open to learning and developing – this should only be done if it makes sense for your charity, if it aligns with the work that you do and if the timing is right. We would not recommend a charity adapting to a funder's interests if those don't match the work, purpose or values of the charity.
>
> Harriet Stranks, Director of Grants, Lloyds Bank Foundation

In practice, achieving a balance between your needs and a funder's needs isn't always so straightforward. Some funders consider themselves programmatic experts and wish to have a lot of involvement in programme design. Some may even prefer to co-develop a project proposal with you, so that it aligns with both your and their charitable objectives. Where this is mutually beneficial and your organisation would still be carrying out the work that was originally intended, this is not necessarily a problem and can indeed bolster the funder relationship. Caution must be taken, however, if the funder's wishes begin to stray from your organisation's wishes and you end up committing to something you didn't actually want to do. In this situation, the key is to be clear about your organisational priorities and set boundaries at the outset. Ultimately, the integrity of your work is the priority, and it is much better to regretfully turn down a grant than to lose control of your own programmatic activities.

A related issue can arise internally where there is lack of clarity about whether a specific project will go ahead and thus whether there is a need to seek funding for it. Many fundraisers have experienced the frustration of being provided with a loose early project design, identifying a funding source with a good fit, developing a proposal based on the early project design, but then learning that the project has been pulled and funding is not needed. This is a waste of time and resources, so it is best to stick to finding funders for projects that are already fully designed and have internal sign-off to go ahead.

'Do we need to carry out due diligence on funders?'

In chapter 3 we looked at the importance of flagging any risk factors that come up while you are researching a prospective funder (see page 44) to inform you whether to continue with an approach. This is due diligence: taking steps to ensure that you do not inadvertently engage with a funding opportunity that conflicts with your organisation's values, objectives or reputation.

Charity trustees have a legal duty to protect their organisation, which includes ensuring that due diligence is carried out on sources of financial support.[4] This is particularly the case for significant funders, although due diligence is recommended where possible at any level of grant.

Many charities have a policy for ethical fundraising. This document should outline which sectors are considered to pose a conflict of interest should any funding be received from them. For example, a charity that works with people affected by addiction might have an ethical fundraising policy that excludes accepting funds from any funder connected to the gambling industry. There are also general reputational considerations, such as if a significant individual at a grant-maker has received negative media attention. In this case, a decision may need to be made as to whether a grant from this funder would pose a reputational risk to the charity by association.

One of the challenges here is deciding how closely connected with the ethical concern a funder needs to be to disqualify a grant opportunity. For example, if a charitable trust derived its income directly from the dividends of an alcohol company, a charity working with people affected by alcoholism might well decide that receiving funding from the trust would be a conflict. But, if the trust's income were received from a range of investments that included shares in a company linked to the alcohol industry, the charity would have to make a decision about whether or not this conflict was distant enough so as not to be a problem.

It is well worth setting up an internal panel, including relevant senior staff, where such cases can be reviewed and an executive decision made on whether or not to proceed with a funder approach. Depending on the size and complexity of your organisation, this panel may include representatives from your finance, communications and programme teams, your executive board and your trustee board – or it might just include some of your trustees.

If due diligence is carried out at the research stage, this will be well in advance of any approach being taken. It can thus save embarrassment on the parts of both the charity and the funder if the relationship cannot proceed. Occasionally, however, an ethical conflict may come to light after a grant has already been received. In this scenario, the internal panel will need to make a decision about whether the funding should be returned. This will depend on how long ago it was received and any other pertinent factors relating to the situation, such as the gravity of the conflict. When a grant is turned down or returned, it can be difficult to explain to a funder why you unfortunately cannot (or can no longer) accept the money. Providing your ethical fundraising policy as an official document can help to diffuse any personal offence. Additionally, if the relationship is significant, it may be appropriate for a senior member of your organisation to provide the explanation. It is ultimately the protection of your organisation that will need to take precedence, even if there is an unfortunate and awkward conversation to be had.

A separate issue – but related to your ethical fundraising policy – is your organisation's environmental impact policy, which outlines the steps taken to work in an environmentally responsible and sustainable way. This area is increasingly of interest to funders, but it is also worth being aware of any potential clashes between your own organisation's policy and activity in this area and that of a prospective funder, which could potentially become an ethical conflict. (The Chartered Institute of Fundraising provides very helpful guidance titled *Environmental Change: A toolkit for fundraisers*.)[5]

'What's the best way to manage small trusts?'

The definition of a small trust can be subjective, but, for our purposes, this section will refer to funders that give grants of under £5,000 as small. Such grant-makers are often under-rated as an important income source.

Even for large grant-seeking charities, this can be the 'bread and butter' income – reliable and cumulatively valuable funding – and it needs to be managed well. Ideally, small trusts should sit under the remit of the grants fundraising team or individual, rather than under direct marketing or a different department, even if the individual grant levels might not seem significant. Grant-makers of any size should have as much of a relationship-based approach as possible, and you should ideally engage with small trusts in the same way as you should with a larger grant-maker. That is, tailor propositions to their individual interests and thank and steward them as valued funders. The tricky thing is finding the time and resources for this level of relationship management, which gets harder the more funders you have to manage.

One solution is to set up a small trusts mailing programme. In general, mailing systems for grant-makers should be avoided like the plague, as you might have anticipated from the past eight chapters' worth of information on bespoke relationship development. However, in this instance, it is better to have a well-thought-out and highly tailored mailing system than not to be managing and maintaining small trusts relationships at all. A mailing system might use your database, or a simple Microsoft Excel spreadsheet, to create a list of funders' names and interests (such as by geography or location) and their giving history to your organisation (new prospect, lapsed funder or current funder; see page 26 for more on these categories). You can then use a mail merge to input this information into the appropriate slots of a pre-prepared proposal. Great care needs to be taken with this method and someone will still need to proofread for any errors in the final documents, but it can be an effective way of producing a large number of similar small trust applications. You will also need to regularly monitor and update the list according to the responses received, and bespoke thanking (calls, emails and letters) should still happen no matter the size of the grant, to ensure that you still undertake the best possible funder care.

National charity Sue Ryder has successfully implemented such a system and has seen the value of nurturing relationships with small trusts:

> So many charities will have trusts that give £1,000 or £2,000 every year. Looking at these trusts' accounts may suggest they don't have the potential to give more, and it is easy to take them for granted. We personalise our small grants programme, phoning to thank for every gift and handwriting thank-you notes. We send small trusts a biannual newsletter tailored around the hospice that the trust has supported and plan surprise gestures, such as delivering cakes to a local solicitors' office that administers several trusts that support us. Recently, one of these small trusts was spending out (giving more as its capital decreased) and got in touch to arrange a grant of £110,000.
>
> Andy Watts, former Head of Trusts, Sue Ryder

Some of these small trusts will require specific application forms or a level of detail that would take up a lot of time and resources. In these cases, it is up to you to determine whether the level of potential grant is worthwhile – if the proposal would cost more (in terms of time, the fundraiser's salary and associated resources) than it would raise, then it is not worth making the approach.

Getting around grant-seeking limitations

'How do we raise funds for unpopular projects?'

There are two schools of thought about how best to approach funders for 'hard-to-fund' projects or causes. The first is to seek alternative funding, such as asking for general funds and then attributing these grants to less popular projects, charging fees for services or diversifying into other income streams. The onus here is on the organisation to find other ways to raise more unrestricted income, which can then be allocated to these particular projects.

The second school of thought – and the one this section champions – is to consider more closely how to frame the proposition. A project might not sound particularly engaging on the surface, but what is the crux of the issue you are addressing? What are the stories behind the beneficiaries that could bring a seemingly dull project to life? Even changing the language of a project or cause can dramatically alter the way it is perceived. For example, a project focused on educating local service providers on users' rights might not sound very exciting; however, when it is repositioned as being the difference that enables a single parent to provide food and shelter for their children, the emphasis shifts on to a more relatable and appealing funding proposition. Some causes and projects may have a grittier exterior, but it is often this kind of work that is actually attractive to grant-makers: the fact that the grant could make a significant difference to a lesser-known, lesser-supported cause can be positioned as a strength.

Changing Faces, a charity working for people with visible differences, has found grant-makers to be particularly interested in supporting causes that are considered more challenging to fund from other sources:

> We find that there's an increasing appetite amongst grant-makers for hard-to-fund, unique causes. At Changing Faces, the fact we're the only organisation for people with all types of visible difference really resonates with funders and some are even keen to fund our campaigning work, which is traditionally thought of as difficult to fund, because they're interested not just in service delivery for individual people but in fundamental societal change.
>
> Sue Canderton, Head of Philanthropy, Changing Faces

Alongside reworking your proposition, you can take a look at the credibility and reputation-building areas covered in chapter 4 (see page 59). Doing this is beneficial for all organisations but especially those that are less known or less understood. Take a step back to consider ways of raising your organisational profile, particularly within the grant-making community, to increase your chances of getting onto funders' radars.

'How do we engage funders with projects they can't visit?'

Chapter 5 looked at maximising engagement and bringing funders as close to your work as possible. Project visits, events and meetings with beneficiaries are a fantastic way of providing this first-hand account, but for some charities the nature of their work makes this difficult. For example, for projects that are far away or overseas, or involve sensitive work, it can be more challenging to engage with funders, as in-person experiences will be impossible or inappropriate.

International Justice Mission (IJM) is a global organisation working to protect people in poverty from violence and exploitation. Given the both sensitive and global nature of IJM's projects, it is rarely possible for funders to visit the organisation's work in person. Therefore, the IJM team needs to be creative in helping funders to experience what the organisation does in the field:

> One of our fundraisers can often be found carrying a brick in his bag ahead of meetings and presentations with funders. The brick is likely to have been made by a man, woman or child experiencing forced labour slavery in one of South Asia's many brick kilns. These facilities can have hundreds of labourers working 18-hour days making upwards of 20,000 bricks each day. Children as young as three years old are put to work, turning the clay bricks so that they dry evenly in the sun. While explaining the reality of life in these brick kilns, the IJM staff member invites the potential funders to pick up the brick and pass it round. The brick is heavy and leaves a layer of dust wherever it goes. This activity provides a small but powerful insight into the daily reality for millions in our world.
>
> Andy Bevan, Scotland Director, IJM UK

This is also where the 'wow moments' explored in chapter 8 (see page 135) are very effective, both for engaging new funders and stewarding existing ones. There are creative ways of bringing an experience to life for a funder, and these can replace an in-person meeting or service visit and be just as powerful. Props are one way of doing this. For example, international aid charities might give funders a sample taste of a high-calorie therapeutic peanut paste that is used to treat malnourished children. Or a charity might ask someone to look through a blurred lens to demonstrate the impact of living with a particular sight disorder, if meeting someone affected by the condition is not physically possible. The aim is to find other ways of creating the experience for the funder, in addition to the information they can take on board from reading about the project.

'Grants fundraising is only part of my role – how can I best manage my time?'

For many fundraisers, grant-seeking will only be one part of their role, or fundraising as a whole may only be part of their job. Sole and part-time fundraisers juggling lots of different balls need to be extra-effective by prioritising their time.

Your main priority if you are a time-restricted grant-seeker is to focus on your best bets. Chapter 2 explored how to qualify prospects by attributing ratings according to their grant-making capacity and propensity to support your cause (see page 31). Where time and resources are limited, prioritising the top prospects will make sure you are focusing on those that are most likely to reap the greatest reward. With current or lapsed funders, prioritise those with the greatest capacity for future grants or the warmest relationships where repeat grants are more likely. Setting up funding alerts (as explored on page 26) is a good way of reducing your prospecting effort where time is scarce.

It is also worth considering where you can outsource additional support. Volunteers are a fantastic resource to help with proofreading, internal information-gathering, mailing small trusts and researching new funding opportunities. Organisations such as Reach Volunteering (www.reachvolunteering.org.uk) may be able to match you with suitable volunteers, some with expertise in fundraising, if you are looking for additional help. NCVO also provides a list of Volunteer Centres on its website (www.ncvo.org.uk/ncvo-volunteering/volunteer-centres), which offer support at a local level for individual volunteers and volunteer-involving organisations and may enable you to find extra help.

Where there are lots of funder relationships to manage, a pipeline management system can be very helpful. This means using a spreadsheet (a simple one in Microsoft Excel can suffice, but it's even better if you have a database with categories that can easily pull off data on each funder) and noting which point in the approach cycle each funder is currently at. This provides a visual snapshot of how many funders are currently at each stage and, if looked at regularly, where any relationships are stuck at a particular stage (see table 9.2 for an example). If a funder has been stuck at 'engagement' for a long time, for example, you can prioritise pushing them along. Or, if a funder has been through the cycle numerous times and you are yet to see any results, it may be time to park them for a while and focus on more likely prospects.

TABLE 9.2 Example of a basic pipeline management system

1. Identification	2. Detailed research	3. Approach planning	4. Relationship-building (engagement)	5. Proposal development	6. Proposal submission and follow-up	7. Thanking, grant management and stewardship
Funder 1						
	Funder 2					
		Funder 3				
		Funder 4				
			Funder 5			
				Funder 6		
						Funder 7

Overall, the best strategy is to avoid spreading yourself too thinly. It is better to put time and energy into developing a few strong relationships than to send out blanket mailings or use a scattergun approach to apply to many funders without any relationship base. Focusing on quality over quantity is likely to achieve the greater income, as well as protecting your organisation's reputation.

Spotlight: a blissful union

Chapters 1–8 of this book journeyed through the stages of the approach cycle (see figure 1.1), describing the partnership between a grant-maker and recipient charity as a relationship. This should be built on mutual trust and respect, and it must be given time to grow and be nurtured to enable it to be the best it can be. It also requires each party to have an understanding of the other's viewpoint, as the relationship will inevitably develop and change over the course of time.

The Institute for Voluntary Action Research (IVAR) published a research report at the end of 2021 that explored the perspectives and motivations of grant-makers regarding unrestricted funding.[6] As part of their interviews with 12 grant-makers, the researchers found that trusts and foundations have a strong awareness of the power differential in their funder–grantee relationships and that many are actively looking to shift this dynamic towards more equality. The report states that these funders desired to understand what was really needed from grant recipients and how, as funders, they could make a stronger contribution to these needs. For some of the grant-makers interviewed, this included increasing unrestricted funding,[7] and most of the funders agreed that enabling grantees to have greater control over their grant spending would significantly reduce the recipients' organisational risk.[8]

Also in 2021, IVAR issued a call for funders to adopt more open and trusting grant-making practices,[9] in order to make life easier for their grantees. At the time of writing, over 100 UK funders of varying types and sizes have signed up to be part of the Open and Trusting Community of Practice, which sets out eight commitments for grant-makers:

1. Don't waste time
2. Ask relevant questions
3. Accept risk
4. Act with urgency
5. Be open
6. Enable flexibility
7. Communicate with purpose
8. Be proportionate[10]

This is an encouraging shift, suggesting that grant-makers are recognising more of the challenges faced by grant-seekers and adapting to work more effectively alongside them. Similarly, grant-seekers need to continue to understand the perspectives of grant-makers, to support the move towards more positive mutual relationships to achieve shared goals for social good.

The Association of Charitable Foundations welcomes this approach through its Stronger Foundations initiative, which seeks to encourage more effective and ambitious practice by foundations:

> The partnership between funder and funded organisation is incredibly important. Through building an effective relationship and developing processes that support this, grant-makers can help to ensure that the funds they offer have the greatest impact in the long term.
>
> Mutual trust and respect are at the heart of this and both sides need to be clear from the outset about what kind of relationship they want. But grant-makers and grant-seekers also need to recognise their differences. For grant-makers this may mean considering the question 'For whose benefit is our offer of support?' and designing their funding processes, programmes and policies accordingly. And, unlike most personal relationships,

funding relationships will often have a planned end – thinking about the end of the relationship from the beginning is a sign of a considerate partner, not a careless one.

The best funding relationships are those that have mission at their heart – an alignment between the mission of funder and funded that enables both parties to achieve their goals.

Richard Hebditch, Director of External Affairs,
Association of Charitable Foundations

Conclusion

No matter the size, age or focus of your organisation, you will regularly face both internal and external challenges in grants fundraising. Clear communication and collaboration are the keys to overcoming almost any issue, whether with your own colleagues or with funders themselves. In this way, you can work together to achieve your shared aims of making a positive difference in the world.

In a nutshell…

- Internal wrangling over team structure and funder ownership can usually be diffused by finding constructive ways to co-ordinate your internal ways of working. These might involve formal agreements being put in place or simply having conversations with colleagues to clarify your roles and ensure that everyone is working together towards the same goal.
- As grants funding often makes up a significant amount of a charity's income, there can be a lot of expectation placed on this fundraising stream. You might find it helpful to educate your senior leadership on realistic time frames, using a systematic forecasting system based on your previous return on investment (often referred to as ROI) or success rates, and mapping out your funder spread to avoid over-reliance on too few funders.
- Just as with internal challenges, external difficulties with funders can be managed through open and honest dialogue. Charities need to maintain clear boundaries, such as where working with a particular funder could result in a programmatic or ethical conflict.
- Reframing how you present your work can enable funders to grasp issues that are otherwise less popular to fundraise for or more challenging to bring to life with traditional case studies or project visits.
- Grant-makers are increasingly open to helping grant-seekers and establishing mutually respectful relationships. Strong communication is key to creating fruitful and long-lasting funder–grantee partnerships, and to working together as one united sector.

Notes

1 *Funding Social Change: How can grant-seekers and grant-makers collaborate to better serve our communities?* [PDF], KEDA Consulting, 2021, www.kedaconsulting.co.uk/wp-content/uploads/2021/06/keda_consulting_funding_social_change_a4_50pp_V2.pdf, p. 14, accessed 7 December 2021.

2 *Ibid*, p. 16.

3 Cathy Pharoah and Catherine Walker, *Foundation Giving Trends 2021* [PDF], Association of Charitable Foundations, 2021, www.acf.org.uk/common/Uploaded%20files/Research%20and%20resources/Research/Foundation%20Giving%20Trends/ACF179%20Foundation%20Giving%20Trends%202021_Design_DigitalVersion_v3.pdf, accessed 29 December 2021.

4 For more details on the responsibilities of charity trustees, see Mike Eastwood and Jacqueline Williams, *The Charity Trustee's Handbook*, London, Directory of Social Change, 2017 (reprinted 2021).

5 *Environmental Change: A toolkit for fundraisers* [PDF], Chartered Institute of Fundraising, 2020, https://ciof.org.uk/IoF/media/IOF/Policy/environmental-change-a-toolkit-for-fundraisers-(1).pdf?ext=.pdf, accessed 7 December 2021.

6 Liz Firth, Ben Cairns, Richard Hopgood and Keeva Rooney, *The Holy Grail of Funding: Why and how foundations give unrestricted funding* [PDF], Institute for Voluntary Action Research, 2021, www.ivar.org.uk/publication/the-holy-grail-of-funding, accessed 7 December 2021.

7 *Ibid.*, pp. 14–15.

8 *Ibid.*, p. 16.

9 Find out more about IVAR's open and trusting grant-making community by visiting www.ivar.org.uk/flexible-funders.

10 *Towards More Flexible Funding: Practical ideas from open and trusting grantmakers* [PDF], Institute for Voluntary Action Research, 2021, www.ivar.org.uk/wp-content/uploads/2021/06/Towards-more-flexible-funding-IVAR-June-2021-Final.pdf, accessed 7 December 2021.

Index

Page numbers in *italics* refer to figures and illustrations and in **bold** refer to tables.